Dedicated to
O. A. Phillips

C L A S S I C
SUPERCHARGED
S P O R T S   C A R S

B Y   T H O M A S   J .   P E R K I N S

Library of Congress Catalog Card Number 83-62607
ISBN 0-9612268-0-3

First Edition
1984

Published by Paradise Press
5842 Paradise Drive
Corte Madera, California 94925

C O N T E N T S

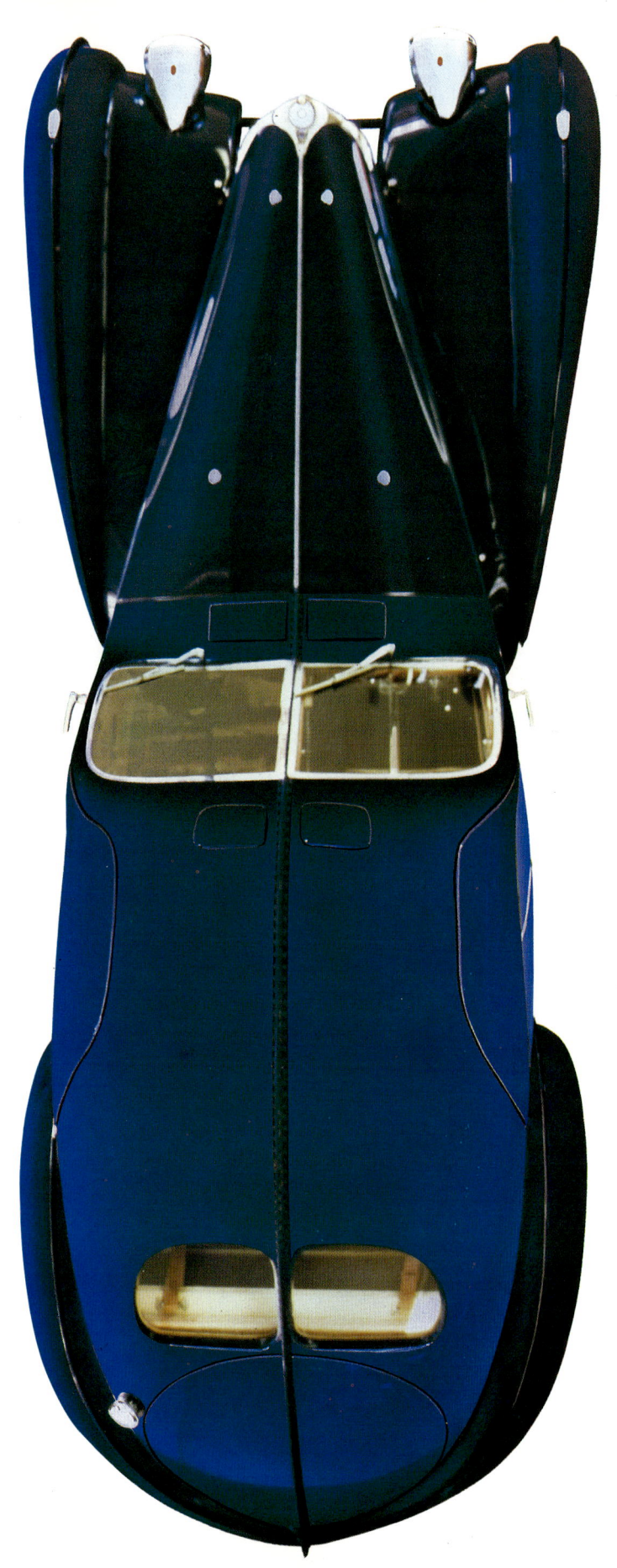

SUPERCHARGED! The word itself is exciting, supercharged with meaning. During the '30s a supercharged sports car was the ultimate possession, desired beyond reason. In Paris a young lady murdered a rich relative to get a Bugatti for her lover! There is nothing in today's world one can buy to deliver as much ego satisfaction pound for pound. A Lear jet won't suffice; a Riva yacht is a pale shadow. Royalty, the rich and the famous enjoyed these luxurious toys produced in tiny numbers and sold at exquisite prices. The cheque for a blown Duesenberg speedster would buy a country estate (it still will). All these beautiful automobiles were outrageous symbols of privilege in a rapidly darkening world. But, with strong racing heritage, they also represented the ultimate in mechanical perfection. And heaven knows, they were great to drive.

Why are these cars collected today when one's extra cash could be applied to acquiring a splendid painting of a soup can or a curiously printed stamp from an obscure country? Well, my view is that automobiles more perfectly capture the psyche of their time than any other art form. Being very complex in design both mechanically and aesthetically, with the automobile there is layer upon layer of opportunity for artistic expression. Moreover, the personality of the producing nation often shows through in fascinating ways. Consider the highly individualistic Bugatti; it could only be French! The English Squire, in typical understatement, hides its flex exhaust pipes under the bonnet, while on the Mercedes they protrude in the most aggressive way. One could go on endlessly discovering these characteristics.

Presented here, then, are photos and personalities of ten of the best supercharged cars of the classic era, drawn from my collection. Each of the manufacturing countries, Italy, France, America, Germany and England, is represented. All the cars are in excellent running order, so the comparisons are made first hand. I wish it were possible in print to capture the feel of an Alfa on the road, the scream of an SSK, or the smell of a Bugatti running on castor bean oil. But these joys along with the choice of the ideal companion for a spin through the countryside must be left to the imagination.

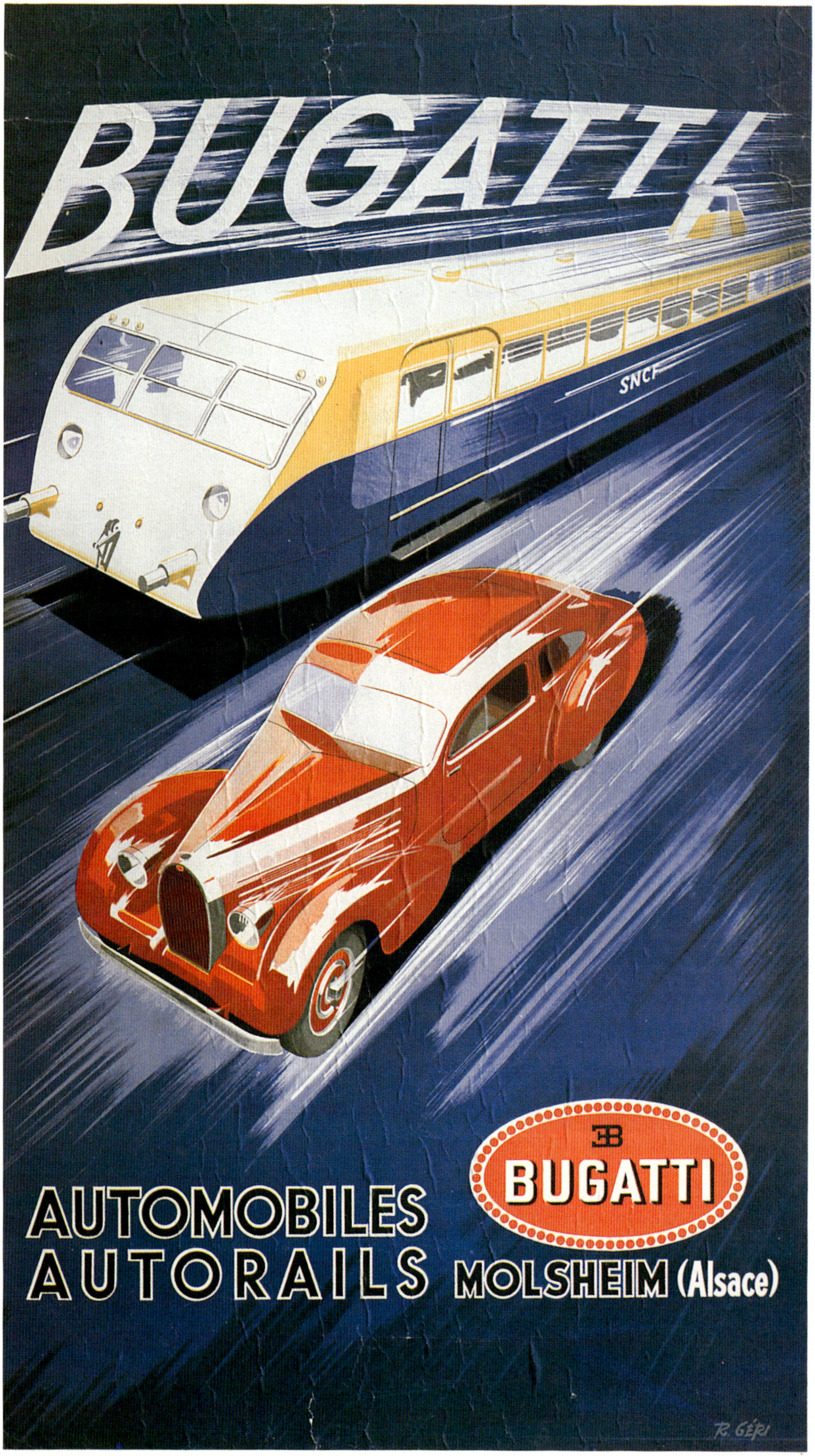
BUGATTI
SNCF
BUGATTI
AUTOMOBILES
AUTORAILS MOLSHEIM (Alsace)
R. GÉRI

*An outstanding design
partnership, Jean and
Ettore Bugatti.*

One does not really *have* to be eccentric with a highly developed taste for the bizarre to own a Bugatti, but it certainly helps and makes one feel in concord with other owners. More than any other marque, Bugatti reflects the complex personality of the designer. The cars are simultaneously exciting and exasperating; they incorporate both brilliant engineering and features of design that could best be called "quaint." They are a pure joy to drive, but alas, maintenance can be awful. For example, on some models to grind the valves you have to start by removing the rear wheels, axle and, working ever forward, extract the engine, crankshaft and pistons at last to expose the little nippers. No Bugatti has a detachable cylinder head, the valve seats are integral with the block in a masterpiece of foundry work and the owner is forever free of blown head gasket problems. The cars are intrinsically interesting, beautiful, even artistic, in every inner detail. There is simply no such thing as a boring Bugatti.

Ettore Bugatti was an engineering artist and a member of an extraordinarily artistic family. His father was a painter and designer of furniture; his brother

Rembrandt was a celebrated sculptor of animals, elected to the French academy in his 20's. Ettore's son, Jean, designed the most beautiful of the cars including the dazzling Atlantic—a triumph perhaps unequaled. But Ettore, the self-taught engineer, also had the personality of a showman and entrepreneur plus the will power to establish the marque as the premier high performance car of France. The works at Molsheim in Alsace carried his stamp in all matters and became a near feudal fiefdom totally unique in 20th century industry. The factory clustered around Bugatti's two chateaus at its pre-World War II zenith, produced nearly all parts of the automobiles, generated its own electrical power and included buildings to house Ettore's thorough-bred horses, his personal collection of coaches and automobiles, and a museum for brother Rembrandt's bronzes. There was even a Bugatti operated hotel nearby for guests, the Hostellerie du Pur-Sang— Inn of the Thoroughbred.

The essence of all things Bugatti Pur-Sang is to be found in the Type 55 roadster of 1932. It was the last car with the mechanical design primarily by Ettore, with little influence from son Jean, and indeed it is an amalgamation of several of his earlier efforts. The chassis is from the Type 54 racing car, the engine from the brilliantly successful Type 51 racer and all the other parts, wheels, axles and so forth from the Type 49 and various other models of the period. The bodies, however, were designed by Jean whose genius for styling greatly exceeded that of his father. Fixedhead and drophead coupes were available, but it was the doorless roadster, as cuddly as a puppy, which captured the sporting personality of the car most perfectly. The aluminum and steel body

In addition to automobiles, Ettore designed and manufactured trains and yachts. His brother, Rembrandt, was a well-known sculptor of animals with a studio at the Antwerp Zoo. Their father, Carlo, was an artist and designer of furniture with intricate copper, bone and aluminum inlays. The unique style was not considered hideous in its day. Ettore even operated his own hotel for important customers.

Ettore Bugatti

panels are strongly sculptured to facilitate the in-variable two-tone paint treatment. The 55 styling is in effect a miniversion of the "Esders" Type 41, the Royale roadster, designed by Jean the preceding year.

With a capacity of 2.3 litres, the 8 cylinder super-charged Type 55 engine produces 135 b.h.p. at 5,500 r.p.m. and a multiplate clutch carries the power from the roller-bearing crankshaft to the mid-frame 4-speed transmission. This arrangement achieves ideal bal-ance, and the handling is excellent although the car is stiffly sprung. The ride may be controlled, how-ever, by the driver via cockpit cable operated ad-justments to the front and rear friction shocks. Acceleration is brisk, zero to 60 m.p.h. in 9½ sec-onds. The top speed is 112 m.p.h.

Two Bugatti powered vehicles, Ettore on the penny-farthing, and the Type 57G, winner of the 1937 LeMans 24 hours.

TYPE 55—SUPERCHARGED ROADSTER

TYPE 55—2.300 LITRE
CHASSIS SPECIFICATIONS

Number of Cylinders...........	8	Body Space........	74″
Bore............	2 3/8″	Overall Size.......	162″ x 60″
Stroke..........	4″	Wheels...........	Cast Aluminum Well Base Rims
Displacement.....	137 cu. in.	Tires............	29 x 5.00
Valves Per Cylinder, Operated by Twin Overhead Camshafts......	2	Weight (approx.)....	2016 lbs.
Number of Engine Bearings........	5	Gas Tank Capacity (approx.).........	22 gals.
Ignition........	Magneto	Gas Consumption (approx.)........	17 M.P.G.
Carburetor......	Zenith	Oil Consumption (approx.).........	800/1000 M.P.G.
Gear Ratios......	1st 9.5–1 2nd 7–1 3rd 5–1 4th 4.15–1	Minimum and Maximum Speed on Top Gear.......	12/110 M.P.H.
Back Axle Ratio..	13 x 54	**PRICE** Delivered New York City............	$7,525
Wheelbase.......	108″		
Track...........	49″		

ACCELERATION REPORT

From Standstill to 60 M.P.H..............	9.5 Secs.
Do Do 80 M.P.H..............	24.55 Do
Do Do 90 M.P.H..............	27.7 Do
Do Do 110 M.P.H..............	53. Do

Additional Information and Specifications on Request

THE name Bugatti needs no introduction to motor car enthusiasts. It is synonymous for speed, stamina and all that is latest and best in automobile construction.

With the introduction of the Type 55, one finds a really comfortable supercharged sports model, capable of something like 112 m.p.h. on the road. It is based on the already famous eight-cylinder two-camshaft Grand Prix model racing car that has such a dazzling series of successes to its credit. The compression ratio is, however, a little lower and other small modifications have been made so that the Type 55 can be run by the ordinary sports car driver with the minimum of maintenance.

As a result, here is a really comfortable, well-sprung car with superlative road-holding characteristics and a performance that is altogether exceptional. It is ideal for travelling safely from point to point at really high speeds and in complete comfort.

Original sales literature for the Type 55 from the American distributor, George C. Rand. Because of the very high price, only a few were sold.

∽ P A R T I C U L A R S   O F   O T H E R   B U G A T T I   C A R   T Y P E S   S U P P L I E D   O N   A P P L I C A T I O N ∽

Jean Bugatti, shown here at age 20, was already an active designer.

The Type 57 was the last important model; it was largely Jean's creation. His brief but brilliant career ended in a fatal crash testing a Bugatti racing car at age 30 shortly before the outbreak of World War II.

The Type 55 Bugatti incorporates Ettore's patented cast aluminum wheels first introduced in the Grand Prix Type 35. The brake drums are integral with the wheel and cooling is exceptional with the spokes acting as whirling heat radiators. The disadvantage, of course, is hot tires and possibly shortened tread life. But tires are a minor maintenance problem compared to the engine which must be re-rollered *every* 5,000 miles. Neglecting these trifles, the Type 55 is a paragon of sports car virtue, but at £1,350 in 1932 it was very expensive. Only 38 of all body styles were manufactured; about 14 remain today. They are highly cherished.

The photographs show the collection's Type 55 roadster. With this model and its incessant demand for expensive overhauls, engine swapping was common in the days before skyrocketing values made the practice impractical. Of the 14 cars remaining, to the best of my knowledge only 3 still have exactly the original chassis and engine as delivered. My car exchanged engines with a mate sometime in its earlier history. At this time of writing, the engine is about to come out again, you guessed it, to be re-rollered!

In 1934 the Type 57 was introduced, and it remained in production until the war ended the Bugatti era. The 57 was greatly influenced by Jean Bugatti's thinking; he was in his mid-20's at the time. The suspension retained the classic forged front axle and the traditional quarter elliptic springs at the rear, but the engine was basically new with improvements throughout. It was very reliable and relatively maintenance-free for one thing, even by the standards of other marques, and secondly, it achieved a very high power per litre: 138 b.h.p. at 4,800 r.p.m. for the 3,257 c.c. basic engine; only Alfa Romeo did better with their 2.9.

A short chassis variation, the Type 57S was introduced in 1935, a very low-slung sporty version of the normal 57. The low profile was achieved by having the rear axle pass directly through the frame. The 57S engine developed 175 b.h.p. at 5,500 r.p.m. with a number of innovations including higher compression pistons, magneto ignition, dual plate clutch and dry sump. In 1937 a supercharger was made available for all models, thereby generating the 57C (for *compressor*) and the 57SC with 160 b.h.p.

Legend has it that Ettore Bugatti responded to a customer complaining about hard starting in cold weather with: "If you can afford a Bugatti, you can afford a warm garage in which to keep it."

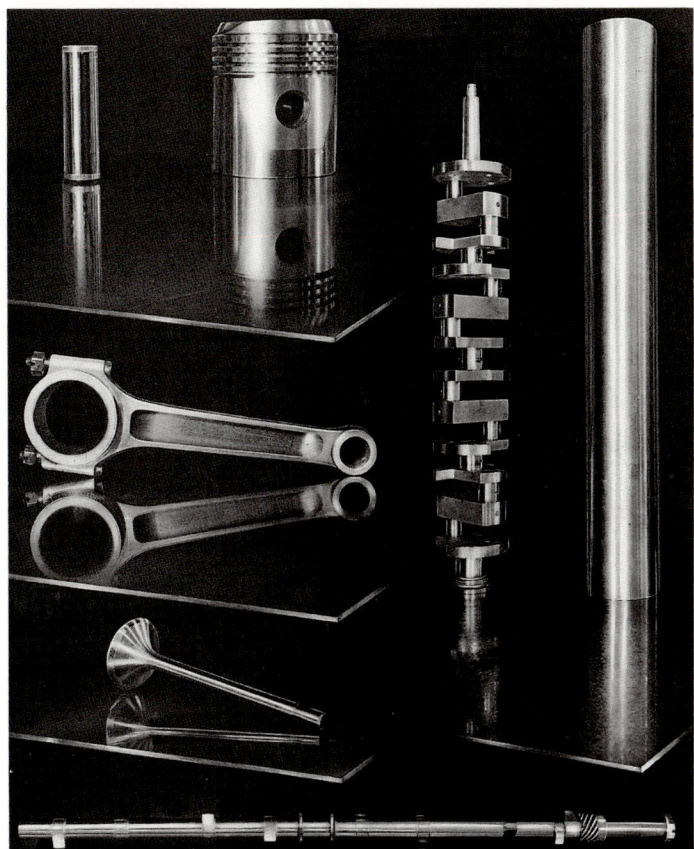

BUGATTI

TYPE 57

3 ᴸ 300

ETTORE BUGATTI — MOLSHEIM — BAS-RHIN

Bugatti sales literature emphasized that the crankshaft was machined from a solid billet. Note also the elegant front axle forging permitting the springs to pass directly through.

Complex deRam shock absorbers are designed into the engine mounting casting on the "top of the line" 57S model. These devices, plus two more on the rear axle, automatically adjust the ride to suit the conditions of the road. Each cost more than a Ford!

for the former and 200 b.h.p. for the latter. The Bugatti Type 57SC was the ultimate pre-war exotic French sports car. Unfortunately, they were terribly expensive to produce and about 40 57S and 57SC cars in total were manufactured. Amazingly, 34 of these masterpieces still exist.

Jean Bugatti emerged during this period as one of Europe's most influential designers. The Atalante (named for the Arcadian princess who agreed to marry the suitor who could outrun her) was one of his most attractive efforts. This beauty doubtless provided the inspiration for the post-war Jaguar XK 120 coupe. About 30 of these bodies were manufactured by the Bugatti shops between 1934 and 1937; in all roughly 670 Type 57's of all body styles were made. The Atalante pictured here was Jean Bugatti's personal car. That it survived his ownership is surprising for Bugatti *fils* had a penchant for racing on the open road, at night and in dense fog. He did this repeatedly. The car ultimately wound up in the United States for restoration by Overton Axton ("Bunny") Phillips. Mr.

Sales literature for the Type 57 Atalante.

The Atalante coupe was another Jean Bugatti design. This example was his personal car.

Coupé

ATALANTE

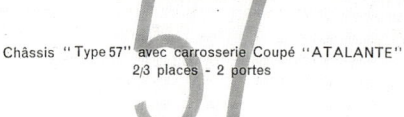

Châssis "Type 57" avec carrosserie Coupé "ATALANTE"
2/3 places - 2 portes

SPORTS MODEL

8-CYLINDER . . . .
3.300-LITRE TYPE 57.S

"SPORTS" 2-SEATER · · · · · ·

A Sports Model introduced to meet the growing demand for a high efficiency car suitable for fast touring or for competing in "Sports Car" racing events including those held under the rules of the A.I.A.C.R. International Sporting Code.

BUGATTI

Chassis specification
overleaf

Original sales literature for the Atalante.

Phillips, former Indianapolis racer, now in his 70's is the world's foremost Bugatti expert. The Atalante underwent a three-year treatment at his hands, emerging not only a Pebble Beach Concours d'Elegance class winner (1981) but hotter on the road than most cars off today's assembly lines.

Both the SC models in the collection started life as 57S versions and were converted to the SC configuration by the factory when the supercharger became available. The roadster has been nicknamed "Bluebird" because it was originally ordered by Captain Sir Malcolm Campbell, the famous land and water speed record holder, and is painted the same color as his renowned Bluebird record cars and boats. Campbell bought the bare chassis from Molsheim and had this one-off lightweight all aluminum body mounted in London by the coachbuilding firm of Corsica. At a total weight of only 2,300 lbs. with 200 b.h.p. available, the performance is shattering.

Sir Malcolm Campbell had his Type 57S bodied by Corsica of London. It was promoted in sales material of the period, but only one was produced.

Campbell wrote at the time, "It cannot fail to attract the connoisseur, or those who know how to handle the thoroughbred. It is a car in a class by itself."

Unfortunately for Sir Malcolm, his enjoyment of his new car was cut short. After only 600 miles of ownership he was elected head of the British Institute of the Motor Trade Inc. and was advised that the lovely new French Bugatti was an unseeming possession. Apparently a true Scot and never quick to pay his bills, he returned the car to the Brixton Road London Bugatti agency and the roadster was sold as a new car to R. E. Gardner, Jr., Esq. Mr. Gardner lovingly maintained the Bugatti for nearly 40 years before the car passed to vintage car racing driver Neil Corner and then to California. This attractive automobile has never been "restored" and has an incredibly low 15,000 miles on the odometer; it won its class at Pebble Beach in 1980.

At the London Motor Show of 1936, the Jean Bugatti-designed *Atlantic-Electron* was unveiled. *Electron* was the then favored term for magnesium alloy, and it was the original intention to manufacture the body from this light metal. Magnesium is hard to weld, so the idea of riveting the body panels arose. Aluminum was finally the actual material used, but the design remained as planned. Jean, making a virtue of necessity, exaggerated the rivet concept, as shown here, into a vehicle straight from the pages of Jules Verne. The riveted fins give an austere, vaguely military aspect, which is then softened by the gracefully curving lines thereby creating a haunting tension. The doors, with their semi-ellipsoidal windows, are deeply carved into the roof and open at a rakish angle reminiscent of aviation styles. The Atlantic, a streamlined masterpiece, was of course too far ahead of its time and only 3 cars were ever sold; all still exist. It is now considered perhaps the most beautiful Bugatti and one of the classic automotive sculptures of all time.

The three Atlantics differ slightly in their design, one having been totally reconstructed after a tragic accident with a train and another having been modified in America after World War II. The third car, shown here, is entirely original. It was ordered by the English tennis champion and Bugattist, R. Pope in 1937, his tenth new Bugatti. A tall man, Mr. Pope

ATLANTIC

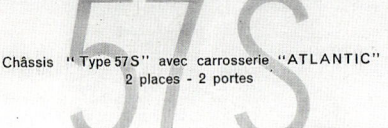

Châssis "Type 57S" avec carrosserie "ATLANTIC"
2 places - 2 portes

PUISSANCE

The Winged Victory of automotive sculpture, Jean Bugatti's masterpiece, the type 57S Atlantic Electron.

negotiated with Jean Bugatti to add one inch to the height of the coupe roof, a nontrivial task requiring new wooden "bucks" to be made for the roof section for use by the panel beaters. He took delivery in 1938 and had the supercharger added in 1939. Mr. Pope, a charming man now in his 80's, assisted me in verifying details of the restoration after the car emmigrated from the U.K. to California.

Ettore never agreed to an independent front suspension, in spite of pressure from Jean. He did, however, innovate with a most unusual front axle design for the 57S. The axle is made in two sections which are screwed together into a common sleeve in the center. The axle halves are able to rotate "independently" within the constraints of a complicated linkage to change slightly the castor angle of the kingpins. This wild idea combined with the wonderful deRam shock absorbers at all four corners gives the 57S models an extremely lively and

A normal Type 57 beside the very low slung Electron.

sensitive feel. The complex deRams incorporate a motion actuated hydraulic pump which works quickly to stiffen or ease the ride automatically to accommodate changing road surfaces. An internal bleed valve adjusts the response time of this apparatus. Each deRam at the time cost more than a Ford.

One doesn't simply jump into a Bugatti and drive off. The engine must be warmed until the oil reaches operating temperature; for the 57SC cars with their dry sumps and 3½ gallon oil reservoirs this takes about 10 minutes. It's worth the wait because on the

road they drive beautifully. The roll center is well below the tire tops so cornering is virtually flat with basically neutral and very quick steering. Overall handling is best for the 57SC models and second only to that of the 2.9 Alfa. The transmissions are 4-speed but with primitive synchromesh (dog clutches), so shifting must be deliberate and double clutching is essential on the way back down. The Bugatti clutch whether single or dual plate is very positive and reliable. The brakes have very large areas with finned drums and stop the car without fuss in modern traffic.

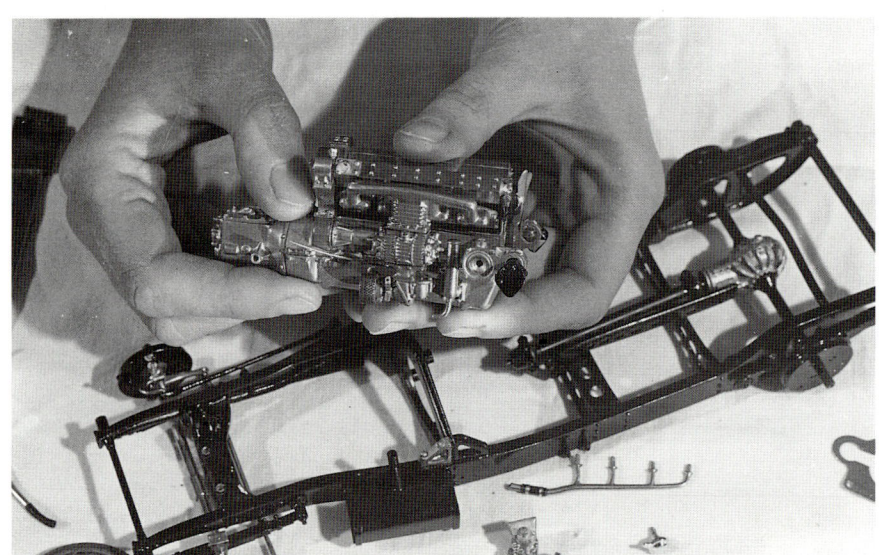

Model builder, Gerald Wingrove of England, has faithfully captured the Atlantic in 1/15 scale. The characteristic Bugatti design elements of quarter elliptic springs at the rear and front springs passing through the axle may be noted. On the few 57S cars produced, the rear axle passes through the frame achieving a low profile.

However, those Bugattis with mechanical brakes experience enough chassis flexure on rough surfaces to make the system rather jumpy, considerably adding to excitement during a fast stop.

With, or perhaps because of, their many eccentric ways Bugattis are the most fun of all the classic supercharged sports cars. They are absolute devils to maintain and repair; Ettore even made his own uniquely sized nuts and bolts and finding the right spanner can be a problem. But they are so audacious—somehow they seem to be *alive*. Bugattis are the easy favorite of any collection.

Cockpit of the Electron. Bugatti typically had two manual controls on the dash, the long levers on the right. One is for ignition advance, the other locks the throttle in any given position—sort of primitive "cruise control."

MERCEDES-BENZ

Hitler, Göring and Eva Braun must have been epic collectors of cars judging from the number of blown Mercedes-Benzes which show up these days advertised as having belonged to them. But the two cars shown here are definitely not from their garage. Would you believe that one is the true "Bonnie & Clyde death car"? Neither would I. Nevertheless, these classic cars are Wagnerian in impact and have unique and interesting histories.

Unlike the design of other supercharged cars, the Mercedes-Benz blower is mounted ahead of the carburetors and is engaged at will by the driver. The advantage of this method is not clear. Perhaps it helps excessive overstressing of the engine, as the owner is warned in several ominous passages of the instruction book to use the 50% increase in power available through the blower very sparingly. This method of dealing with supercharging adds enormously to the complexity of the design. When the supercharger is engaged by depressing the accelerator beyond the normal full open, a special clutch (actually a series of metal discs) actuates the Roots

The mighty SSK engine with standard blower at the front. The "Elephant" blower is considerably larger. A creation of Dr. F. Porsche, the massive motor incorporates a second oil sump at the rear of the block which further adds to its bulk.

type rotors; a special valve switches the air flow from normal atmospheric pressure to supercharged pressure, and another set of carburetor jets is employed. At the same time, the gas tank is pressurized to assist fuel flow to the gulping engine; not economy cars these, while blown 5 m.p.g. is typical. All this action is accompanied by an ear-splitting banshee scream from the blower. This sound is very intimidating, and one is sensibly advised by the owner's manual to "drive very cautiously on encountering frightened animals."

The top photo shows the normal SSK chassis, the lower the SSKL created by drilling out 250 lbs. of steel from the frame. The brute strength of these designs is awesome, indeed.

When the accelerator is released the blower must stop instantly, which requires a second set of metal disc braking plates, and everything flops back to normal. Mercedes-Benz stuck to this method of supercharging in spite of the complexity until the latest Grand Prix cars immediately before the Hitler war. Undoubtedly the market appeal of the blower's Valkyrie screech was the compelling reason.

The supercharged cars were a small fraction of the factory output, being sold to movie stars, aristocratic amateur racers and the like. The blown cars were in effect advertising to pull the bread and butter production vehicles through the marketplace. Of all the S series only 149 S, 114 SS, 31 SSK and 7 SSKL autos were produced; however, the factory team racing SSKLs were not sold to the public. Of the glamorous 500K and 540K series, only 700 of all body types were built. The S stands for *sportmodell*, and the second S for *super*, the L for *licht*, the K stands for *Kurtz* in the SSK and *Kompressor* in the 500K series (confusing, *nicht wahr?*).

The SSK shown here is a very, very rare and widely traveled beast indeed. The engine and chassis were designed by the great Ferdinand Porsche but the factory fitted the motor with the giant "Elephant" blower designed by Porsche's successor, Hans Nibel. This massive and Teutonic device was the largest of the three sizes made and reserved ordinarily for the team racing SSKL models. It is likely that less than 10 of these Roots type blowers were manufactured. The "Elephant" boosts to 12 p.s.i., runs at 3 times engine speed, and employs 2 vanes of 2 lobes each. Also fitted to this engine are special alloy cylinder sleeves, extra large valves for optimum breathing, racing type cam and followers, and a special high capacity oil pump. The chassis was made in 1930 and shipped on speculation to Tokyo where a prospective buyer would have had his own sports body fitted as was the custom of the time. No buyer had the yen to come forward, however, and the chassis was returned to the factory in 1932. Count Carlo Felice Trossi of Italy then bought it.

Count Trossi was the quintessential aristocratic motor sportsman of the '30s. He was an amateur racing driver disporting himself with distinction in several pre-war Mille Miglia contests; he provided the financial backing for the young Enzo Ferrari's Scuderia Ferrari racing teams, and he was president of the firm; he underwrote the Trossi-Monaco, a radical radial engine Grand Prix car (which was regrettably a bust), and was overall a connoisseur of automobiles of the first caliber. Trossi, however, must have been a boy at heart — look at the sweeping body he designed for his new SSK! This car, which was built in his shops, anticipated the Green Hornet and the Batmobile by decades. The car is utterly impractical without any storage space at all, not even

Dr. Ferdinand Porsche, designer of the SSK.

Dr. Hans Nibel, designer of the 500K.

a glove compartment — but the lines are spectacular. This is my vote for the world's most beautiful SSK Mercedes-Benz, as well as the fastest.

The car escaped destruction by fleeing to the Count's estate in Argentina where it was alive and well during the war. But after the war the SSK passed through several neglectful South American and American owners until, tired and very shabby, it fell into the hands of a very well-known collector and restorer who has been accused elsewhere of converting SSK models into the more rare factory racing

Engine room aboard the SSK with the "Elephant" blower evident. The austere instrument panel still carries the tach with shift speeds marked by Count Trossi.

*Opposite:
Count Carlo Felice Trossi's SSK Mercedes-Benz.*

SSKL Type. The SSKL was nearly identical to the SSK except that about 250 lbs. of steel was removed by cutting circular holes in the frame. While lightening the car, this Swiss-cheese treatment drastically reduced the strength of the frame. Bogus SSK to SSKL conversions have apparently been done frequently enough so that the authenticity of most SSKLs is suspect. The Trossi car survived and was subsequently acquired by Anthony Bamford, the famous U.K. collector, who supervised a complete restoration in England before the car crossed the

Atlantic once again (this time in the belly of a jet) to find its new home in California.

The photos of the engine reveal a ship-sized power plant, beautifully detailed with "engine turning" on all the shiny parts. It would be quicker to describe the plots of the four "Ring" operas than to cover the approximate workings of this engine design. The owner's manual, for example, requires 14½ pages just to explain the theory of operation of the supercharger and two carburetor combination. I'll touch on only the lubricating system, which is among many

The top photo is the normal factory bodied SSK, as Teutonic as the Brandenburg Gate. The Trossi design combines the tension of soft sweeping curves with angular lines to achieve a compelling beauty.

interesting features, and pass over the dual ignition, decompression ports, assorted pumps (including the engine-operated tire inflator) and other exotica.

Never let a friend check the oil level of his SSK in your driveway. The engine, you see, employs two oil sumps and lubricating systems, one for "fresh" oil on top and another sump on the bottom for "circulating" oil. At the start of a trip one fills each with about 8 quarts and, while the miles pass, the engine cunningly administers fresh oil to the lower sump to compensate for the oil being consumed (about one *quart* for every 40 miles if things are working normally). But, if one is having a good day and the consumption is less than predicted, the oil overaccumulates in the lower sump. Your friend thus "checks his oil" by rotating a valve to "MAX" position which immediately dumps the excess on the ground. Alternatively, it may have been a tough trip — perhaps the engine burned up more oil than the metered amount? Easy to tell; just turn the valve to "MIN" and look for more oil being poured on the ground. This may seem unduly complicated, if not downright messy, but it fits perfectly with the overall thrust of Mercedes-Benz design thinking of the period.

The SSK with its 7 litre engine and "Elephant" blower engaged churns out some 300 b.h.p. at the low r.p.m. of 3,300. The torque is fantastic and the gearing is very tall so that the top speed of about 140 m.p.h. is achieved without over-revving. The weight of 3,500 lbs. gives a favorable power-to-weight ratio which makes the performance very exciting and in a straight line better than that of the big Alfa and the Bugattis. But the steering is very heavy and one sits so far aft behind the tremendously long hood that it seems to take a long time for a turn of the wheel to show up as a change of direction. This feeling of massiveness, the heavy-to-operate mechanical brakes and the notorious oversteering tendency, together with the maniacal howling of the supercharger makes one think twice about really putting his beam-axled beast through its paces. While the power-to-weight ratio is superior to the Italian and French rivals and while from history we know the SSK won its share of races, I can only marvel at the accomplishment and at the raw courage shown by drivers as von Brauchitsch and Caracciola. The SSK is intimidating!

The SSK was the last of the hairy-chested Mercedes-Benz sports cars. By the mid-30's, Hitler had started his Autobahn program and the coveted auto was one which would cruise down these well-paved roads in style and comfort. The days of the dust and pebble SSK had drawn to a close. Also, the days of aesthetic functionality in German automobile styling had drawn to a close, to be replaced with the aggressive look of the 500K and the ostentatious 540K follow-on. It has been observed that automobiles are the only new art form of the 20th century and that their design and styling reflects the culture of the producing nation. Certainly, the turmoil developing in the German psyche of 1935 can be visualized today in the chrome and mass of the arrogant 500K Special Roadster. Two and a half tons of steel, 5 or 7 headlights, 3 or 5 airhorns — one can visualize the Baron, or more likely the Nazi party dignitary, blasting the peasant with oxcart inadvertently encumbering the passage of this juggernaut! They had a word for it, *Prunkwagen,* or prestige car; the bigger and more assertive, the better.

The Honorable Arthur Gore must have been an English sports car buff of very thick skin indeed, oblivious to the conditions developing in the Nazi Germany of August, 1935, to have ordered this 500K Special Roadster at all, not to mention its full complement of accessory lights and horns sufficient to bring Sweeney to Mrs. Porter in the spring. The car was one of the very few to be exported to the United Kingdom and fitted with right-hand drive; it still carries its original English registration (CCP 528) and GB letters under the special light provided.

The 500K series utilizes a 5 litre engine of less sophistication than the SSK — push rods instead of overhead cams, smaller supercharger and less efficient carburetion. The power output is 100 b.h.p. in normal operation and 160 b.h.p. with blower engaged. Not much oomph to move 5,000 lbs. of vehicle. On the other hand, the chassis was a breakthrough. It incorporated the new Mercedes-Benz ideas in independent suspension all round and the sales literature of the time correctly heralds this advance in technology as significant and "destined to point the way for automobile technique of tomorrow." The ride of a 500K is excellent. The springing is just right, firm enough for corners but compliant enough for the bumps. Undoubtedly the weight of the car helps in this effect. The brakes are also, fortunately, effective in stopping the progress of this behemoth on schedule. They are hydraulic and servo-assisted with a vacuum boost from the engine. Of all the cars in these pages, the 500K is unquestionably the most comfortable to drive on a trip and, under today's anachronistic speed laws, not really much of a laggard. An honest 100 m.p.h. is within its grasp.

Around a dozen of these Special Roadsters were built; 4 or 5 remain today. This car was purchased

MERCEDES-BENZ

Opposite:
The stuff of which dreams
are made. The 500K
roadster at Pebble Beach
the morning after winning
Best of Show.

in Georgia after a career of considerable travail, traveling several hundred thousand miles for some 10 owners. She was still driveable, and indeed I took her on a test run, but so many aches and pains were evident that, had the 500K been a horse, I would have been accused of cruelty to animals for urging it onward. It has now been restored by Autoeuropa down to the last nut and bolt and is in concours condition (Best of Show, Pebble Beach, 1982). This was a task of more than the usual difficulty because of the great complexity of the type. While a restoration of this magnitude is really a challenge, it is also fun to scout out parts and advice from around the world; you make many interesting acquaintances. However, there is little help to be had from the factory; they advise merely that the defeat in the second World War interferes with their normal service programs.

The SSK and 500K Mercedes-Benz supercharged sports cars have a ponderous personality unique among all automobiles. Honestly, they are not the most mechanically advanced or quite the most fun to drive. But, they are reliable beyond measure, demanding, and truly exciting. They seem to say "you *will* enjoy me"...and you do!

From the 1935 factory
catalogue.

MERCEDES-BENZ TYPE 500 SUPERCHARGED   SPECIAL ROADSTER • 2-4 SEATS

ALFA ROMEO

Young Vittorio Jano beside his victorious P-2.

As there are glamorous and exciting women who will make you into a *real* man, the classic Alfa Romeos will make you into a *real* driver, and probably be more trustworthy to boot. Alfa has won the Mille Miglia eleven times, more than all the other marques' wins combined, in this 1,000 mile classic, the toughest of all road races. Throughout its long history, Alfa Romeo has more perfectly combined superb sports car handling with mechanical stamina than any other competitor. While the two cars presented here bracket the '30s decade, each is a masterpiece and a pure joy to drive, though vastly different one from the other.

The 1750 (officially the 6C1750) Alfa Romeo was one of the most successful sports cars ever made and the first to be "mass" produced. Introduced in 1929, it remained in production through 1933 and was available with and without blower in both Gran Sport and Gran Touring configurations. In all, some 2,579 of all types were manufactured, including about 320 Gran Sports. The most beloved of all was the Zagato-bodied supercharged, short chassis Gran Sport model, one of which is part of this collection.

This car makes its first good impression by virtually bursting into life when the starter button is pushed. In an era when other makes could be horribly balky (Bugatti comes to mind), the 1750 never fails to fire immediately even in cold weather. The engine has a very fast idle, about 1,500 r.p.m., and quickly comes up to operating temperature. The multiplate clutch is very positive (but cannot be slipped or the plates will warp, rendering it inoperable). Underway, the clutch and gearbox work together beautifully provided double clutching is never forgotten. The transmission is integral with the motor, and shifting is facilitated through the classic Alfa "gate"; a hinged cover is swung away to expose the slot for reverse. Once the accelerator location between clutch and brake is mastered, heel and toe sports driving becomes second nature. The engine loves to rev rapidly and the characteristic Alfa sound, a sharp "rap" imposed upon a gear whine from cam drive and supercharger, is intoxicating.

The 6C1750 is classical in its chassis and springing; that is to say, the springs are virtually inflexible and the chassis rubber-like. It works. Relative motion between the two is somewhat controlled by the large friction "shock absorbers" at the four corners. After one accommodates to the sensation of undulating fenders and totally flexible body work, the car can be driven with near abandon. It is absolutely neutral in corners and extremely forgiving. The

Alfa Romeo 6C1750 sports car bodied by Zagato. The aesthetics of Jano's engine design are equal to Bugatti's.

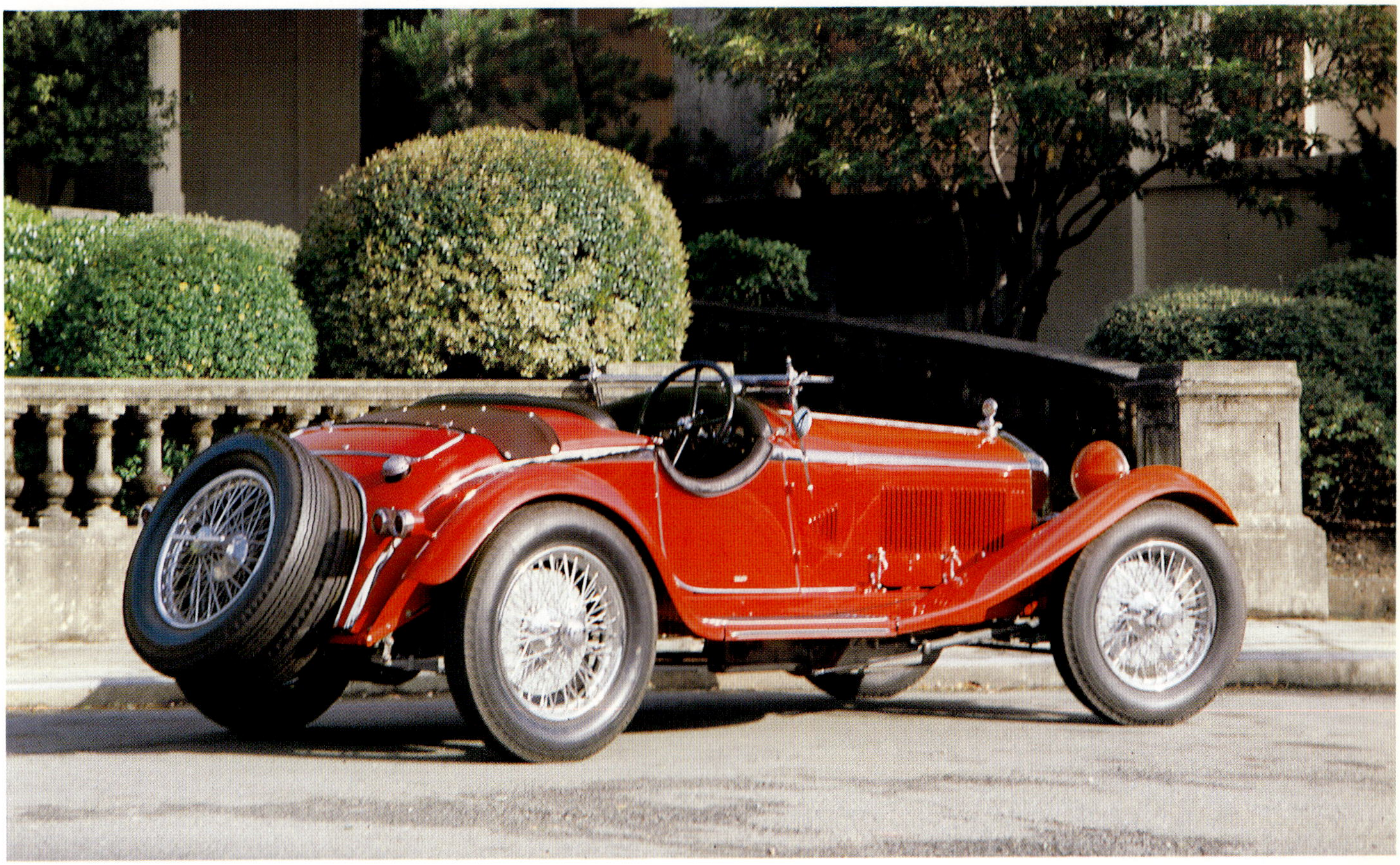

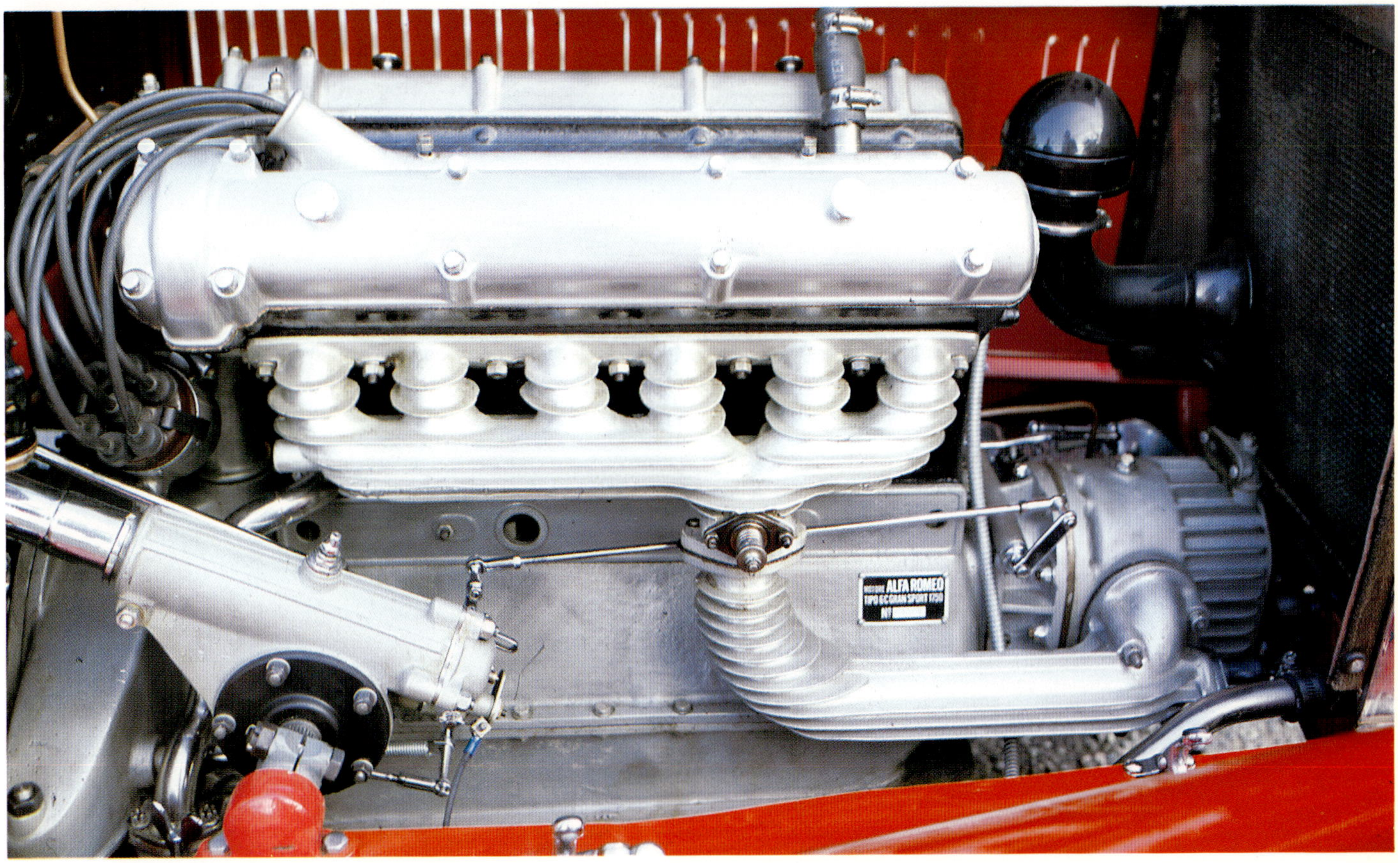
ALFA ROMEO
TIPO 6C GRAN SPORT 1750

ALFA ROMEO

ALFA ROMEO

steering is so quick that steering wheel motion is almost undetectable by the passenger. The driver seems to "think" the car around fast bends and, of course, there is no lean. With such positive steering, clutch, and mechanical brakes to match, even a 6-foot driver doesn't feel cramped in the none-too-roomy cockpit.

The car shown here was born in 1930, which was the never to be forgotten year 4 similar 1750's came in 1st, 2nd, 3rd and 4th in the Mille Miglia in a clean sweep over Mercedes-Benz and Maserati. This was the famous race between the great drivers, Varsi and Nuvolari, who both ignored team instructions and drove like demons against each other for first place. Varsi was in the lead during the dark morning hours, but Nuvolari was gaining. The incredible Nuvolari turned off his lights and raced for miles behind the unsuspecting Varsi, finally to pass him and hold the lead to victory.

So many names of the automotive greats of the '30s found their way on to marques, Bugatti, Duesenberg, Porsche, and of course Ferrari, that they cannot be forgotten. Unfortunately, the man behind Alfa during the '30s, Vittorio Jano, was not so lucky. Yet he was a design genius, perhaps greater than any of the others. Brought to the attention of Nicola Romeo by a very young Alfa racing driver and dealer, Enzo Ferrari, he was hired away from Fiat by Romeo in 1923. Like Ettore Bugatti, Jano was not only concerned with the function of his designs but also with their appearance. Note the details of the inlet manifold shown in the photo and the elegant simplicity of the overall engine compartment.

The Jano 1750 Alfa engine is one of the great automotive masterpieces which helped to establish the supremacy of Alfa in racing for many years. It is classic in its construction with a 5 main bearing crankshaft, pressure lubricated, and unlike the 55 Bugatti, rollers with their reliability problems were avoided. The engine was available with or without removable cylinder head, but the vast majority produced had the detachable head, as does my car, with the ease of maintenance this provides. The dual overhead cams and central spark plug location are classical, and indeed this arrangement in this extremely popular design helped to establish the DOHC layout as optimum. For the Gran Sport model, 85 b.h.p. at 5,000 r.p.m. was achieved which would

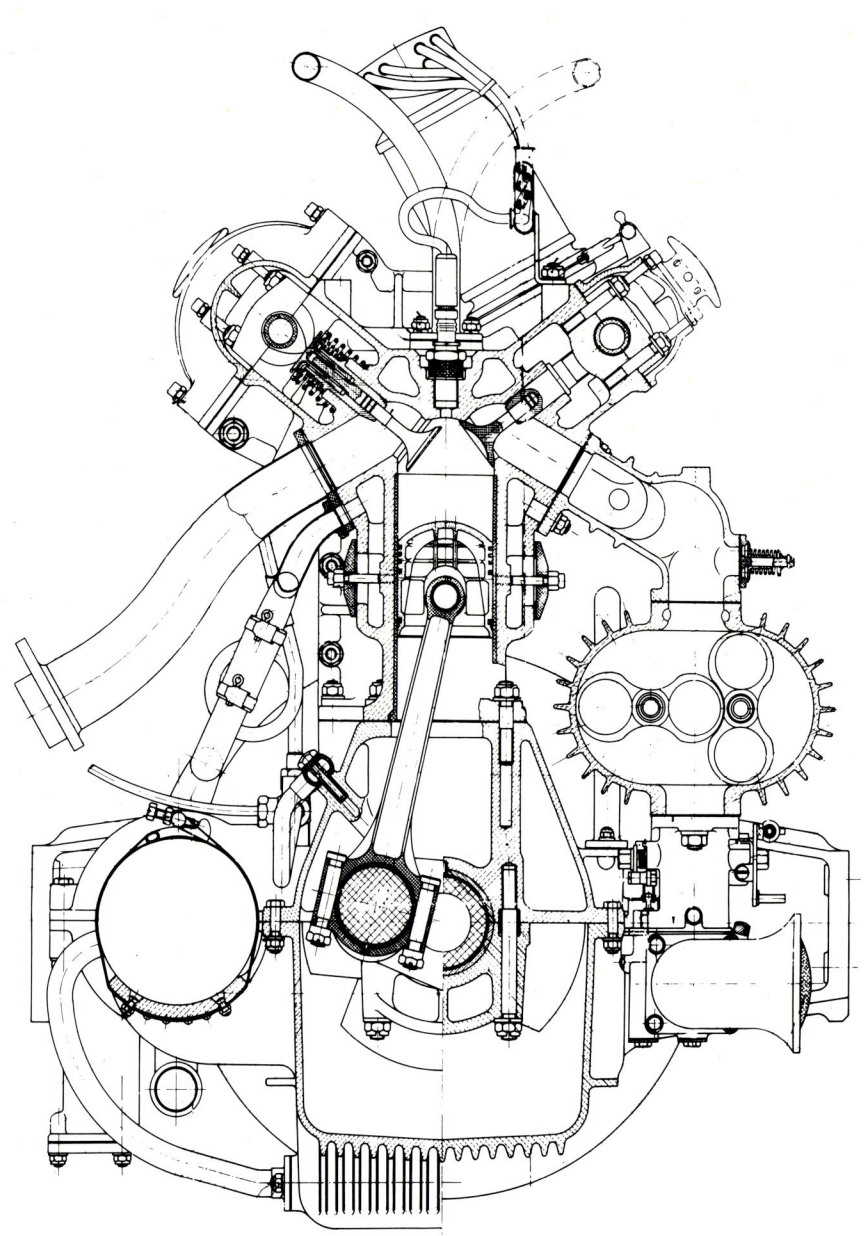

Factory drawings of the 8C2900B engine. Note the construction of the supercharger. The counter rotating lobes sweep air into the engine on each revolution.

propel the car from zero to 60 m.p.h in 13.9 seconds. This is a great deal of power from only 1.75 litres and, of course, the Roots supercharger is responsible. It boosts pressure over 6 p.s.i. or nearly half an atmosphere. Perhaps it is time to comment on supercharging in general.

It was discovered early in the development of the high performance engine that power is ultimately dependent upon the weight of air burnt per minute, and breathing through the aperture of the inlet valve is the limiting factor. By increasing the pressure of the air in the manifold, obviously, more air carrying

The magnificent 8C2900B engine. The generator, oil and water pump are shown in the upper photo. The starter is in the housing at the rear — the transmission is, of course, on the rear axle.

The lower photo shows the two carburetors, two superchargers and two intake manifolds. With magneto, dual overhead cams and dry sump, the design was "state of the art."

ALFA ROMEO

a charge of fuel could enter the cylinder. The higher the pressure, the greater this "supercharge." In 1860 the Roots brothers of America invented the type air pump, which carries their name to this day, for moving air into mine shafts. The key to the design was the external gearing of the two rotors so that they would turn without touching and move a volume of air from input to output on each revolution. The drawing shows how this works. If the tolerances are close, as they should be, there is a minimum of air leakage between the rotors and around the endplates, and the Roots pump is essentially a positive displacement type. Early in this century Roots blowers were adapted to automobiles. It was quickly ascertained that this concept was superior to the centrifugal design which had to build up speed before the boost was evident. Roots blowers are used on all the cars in this collection with the exception of the Duesenberg, which is of the centrifugal type.

Supercharging has been rediscovered today in the form of the turbocharger. The turbocharger has two great advantages over the supercharger; it is cheap to build, and it operates from power that would

*Alfa Romeo 8C2900B
short chassis roadster with
body by Touring.*

otherwise be wasted. It incorporates two centrifugal turbines, one located in the exhaust to provide the power, and the other after the carburetor in the inlet manifold system to boost the pressure. The two turbines are linked by a common shaft. Whereas the supercharger takes its operating power directly from the engine via gearing and requires (depending on boost pressure) roughly 25% of the total power of the engine, the turbocharger takes its power as a heat engine does, by creating an appreciable temperature drop in the exiting exhaust stream. With minimal back pressure on the exhaust, the turbine extracts power by converting heat to work. This heat would normally be wasted down the exhaust pipe and into the atmosphere, so the power for turbocharging is effectively "free." The turbocharger turbines are also relatively simple to manufacture, compared to the precision machining required for Roots rotors, and no gearing is required; thus the turbocharger has a cost advantage over the non-heat efficient supercharger.

The supercharger of the Roots type does, however, retain one great advantage. Since it is essen-

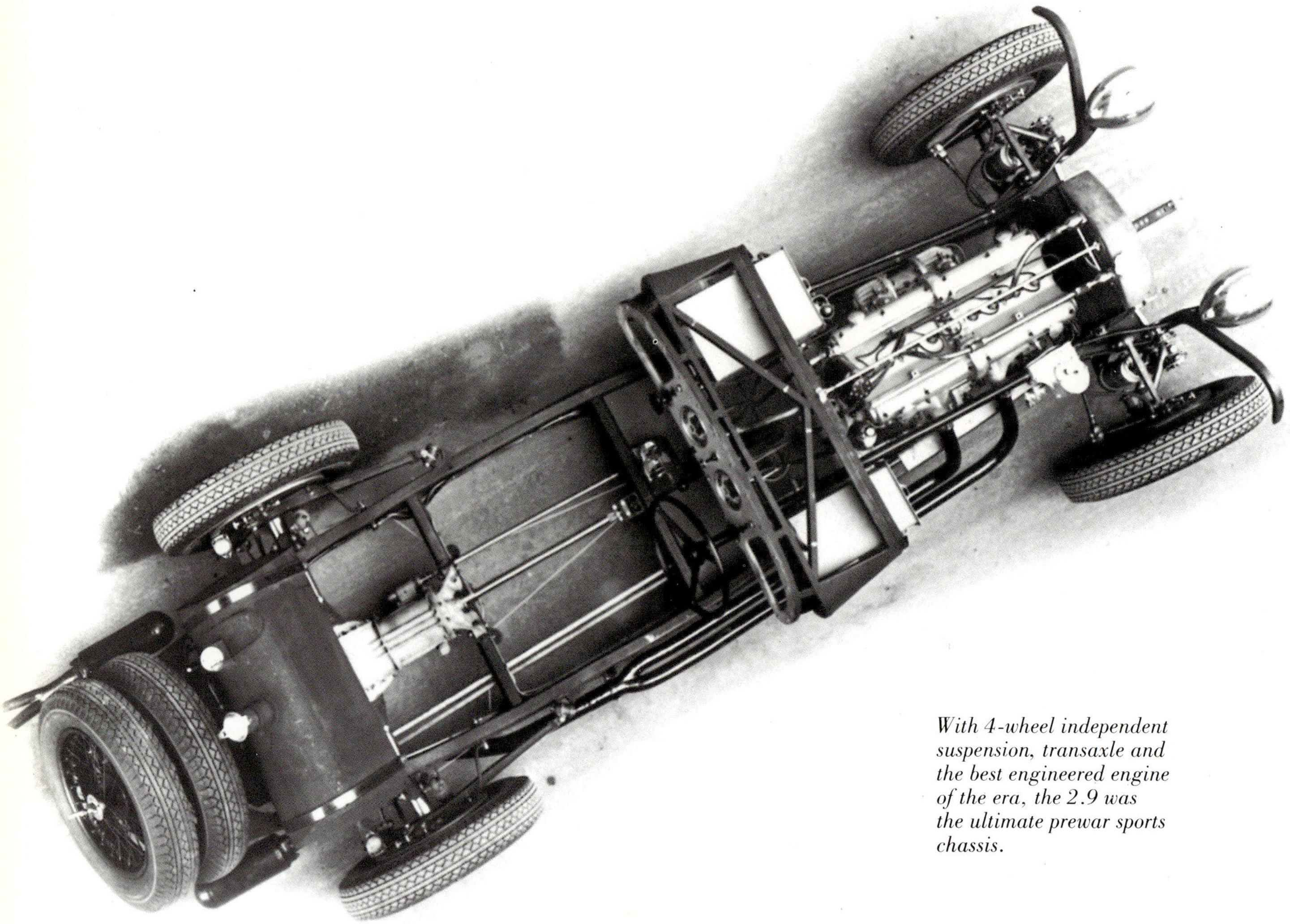

*With 4-wheel independent
suspension, transaxle and
the best engineered engine
of the era, the 2.9 was
the ultimate prewar sports
chassis.*

tially a positive displacement pump, its pressure boost is immediate. The agonizing wait for power build-up known as "turbo lag" does not exist. For sports cars, this is a very attractive feature, possibly worth the sacrifice of significant engine efficiency. One wonders how the great designer Jano would have made the trade-off in his day.

The second Alfa of this collection is the extremely rare 2.9 (officially the 8C2900B), Jano's masterpiece and the ultimate sports car, bar none, of the pre-war period. The design of this 2.9 litre paragon did not at one time emerge Venus-like fully developed, but rather evolved from a series of successful racing types starting at the beginning of the decade. The engine derives from the 8C2300 Monza, which was the first of the Jano Alfa designs where two 4-cylinder blocks with 10 main bearings were combined with a central gear drive between the two, providing power to the supercharger and drive to the two overhead camshafts. Light alloy was used throughout with steel liners for the cylinders; the cylinder head was nondetachable, being integral with the block. In 1932 this design further evolved to the 8C2600 Monoposto. Here for the first time *two* superchargers were incorporated, one for each carburetor, an optimum if expensive solution to efficiency in breathing. Power was increased to 215 b.h.p. from the 178 b.h.p. of the predecessor.

Then in 1934 the bore was again increased to 2,905 c.c. displacement and power boosted to 255 b.h.p. for the famous Tipo B racing car. This machine, which the ever incredible Nuvolari piloted to victory in the

1935 German Grand Prix, was the first to incorporate the all-independent suspension which is used in the 8C2900B. The rear end has swing axles, located by radius arms, telescopic shock absorbers, and the chassis is supported via a transverse leaf spring. The front suspension (also independent) comprises trailing arms with coil springs and telescopic shock absorbers encased in oil-filled cylinders. This combination achieved road-holding power beyond anything of the era and is equally efficient by modern standards.

With all this technology from racing mastered, in 1937 Jano unveiled the culmination of the effort in the sports version, the 8C2900B. The engine was detuned for street use to 180 b.h.p. at 5,400 r.p.m., but magneto, dry sump, twin Weber carburetors, and, of course, dual superchargers were all there. The transmission (4 speed) was incorporated into a rear transaxle, very unusual and advanced, to achieve perfect balance in the vehicle. The huge 19-inch wheels afford the use of very powerful hydraulic brakes. Both long (118 inch) and short (110 inch) chassis versions were available; roadsters and coupes were fabricated by the leading Italian coachbuilding firm, Touring. The term *superleggera*, or ultra light, was coined by Touring for these 2.9's as the coachwork was all metal, stretched over a metal frame in a new technology of lightweight bodymaking which eliminated the wooden subframe entirely. The all-steel bodies are lighter than the aluminum counterparts used by most competitors. The combination of Alfa and Touring achieved a design in which the short chassis roadster version, the car shown here, can achieve zero to 60 m.p.h. in 9.4 seconds with an easy top of 120 m.p.h.

Details of the 2.9 independent suspension: top left, the rear design with transverse leaf spring; upper right, the front with coil spring hidden within the cylindrical damper; the lower photo shows the transaxle and independent half shafts with trailing arms.

Only a total of thirty 8C2900B's were manufactured and sold at the very high price of £2,250 in the two years of production, 1937 and 1938. While many of the cars were similar in body style, no two were exactly alike. They were absolutely the finest sports cars available; nothing really could compare with them. Both Alfa and Touring were receiving government support from the Mussolini regime — Alfa to develop cars to compete with Hitler's Auto Unions and Mercedes-Benzes, and Touring to develop lightweight aircraft structures. It is perhaps not stretching the point excessively to compare the 2.9 Alfa with its advanced technology and the awe in which it was held by the public with today's Space Shuttle which enjoys similar accolades.

The 2.9 shown here was manufactured in 1938 and sold to India for a lesser Maharajah, where during the war it figured as evidence in a sensational murder trial. An RAF pilot brought it to Australia after the war, and for a time it was part of the important Jarvis Alfa collection there. In 1969 Jackson Brooks imported it to America, where after two additional owners it joined this collection. Total use is amazingly only 17,000 miles since new. Just four of these beautiful short chassis 2.9 roadsters remain.

Among the cars in these pages, the 2.9 is unquestionably the best handling and best performing, from any point of view; considering the company it keeps, that is quite an accomplishment. It will make a *real* driver of you for sure.

Vittorio Jano in late years driving a 1750 Alfa Romeo during a rally to honor the marque.

S Q U I R E

Imagine starting your own motor car manufacturing company at 21, with financial backers and directors of about the same age, and coming up with a stunner, a dream car received by the motoring world with rave notices. That's what the young entrepreneur Adrian Morgan Squire accomplished in England in the mid-30's. That was a time when a sophisticated motoring gentry requiring swift sporty cars (*brakes* they called them) to traverse the lovely English countryside supported the development of a number of small quality manufacturers as A.C., Alta, Aston Martin, Bentley, Fraser Nash, H.R.G., Invicta, Lagonda, Lea-Francis, M.G., Riley, Triumph and, of course, the wretched Jaguar. With the exception of the wretched Jaguar, it was a period of exceptional flowering of the sporting marques, never before seen nor equalled since. The handful of Squires produced were the best of the lot.

At 16 Squire began planning his masterpiece; during his school days at Downside, a complete specification for the car was written. Upon graduation, rather than continuing study at a university, he chose a practical course of electrical engineering at a trade school in London and after a year he moved on to Bentley Motors where he worked as an apprentice. This was in 1929 and prior to the take-over of Bentley by Rolls-Royce; W. O. Bentley himself was still in command and young Adrian learned from the master. But Bentley cars were massive affairs; W. O. had, after all, been a locomotive designer. Ettore Bugatti's unsporting observation that "Mr. Bentley is a builder of very fast lorries" was not much off the mark. Squire soon sought automotive experience with the M.G. car company whose sports cars were much closer to his idealized specification. During his two years with M.G. at Abingdon-on-Thames, Squire established himself as an outstanding engineer with sparkling native talent.

At a mature 21, Squire was ready. He obtained financial backing from a young friend, Gage Spicer, heir to a family paper manufacturing fortune, and pooled in his own modest inheritance. Joining him and also investing were 20-year-old Jock Manby-Colegrave (who looked a good 5 years younger than Adrian) and 26-year-old Reginald Slay who was nicknamed "Uncle" by the younger co-founders. Two older mechanics from Bentley's added more talent

The very business-like chassis of the Squire prototype X101 and its engine, from original factory photographs. The finned oil cooler and very strong custom made manganese alloy axle will be noted. In the lower photo, twin water pumps can be seen at the forward end of the cam cover. The deeply finned inlet manifold conducts air from the supercharger hidden behind the radiator. The dual purpose dynamotor is mounted between the dumb irons.

to the team, and the Squire Car Manufacturing Company was established in 1931 in a small garage in the village of Remenham Hill about a mile from Henley-on-Thames, Oxfordshire.

The Squire was intended to be the finest English sports car ever produced and its design required a great deal of time and testing. Only a young idealist striving to realize an earlier dream would have adopted the no-compromise approach, which led to technical triumph (and commercial disaster). In the early days the Squire people covered some expenses by

The young entrepreneurs. Jock Manby-Colegrave and Adrian Squire in front of the Remenham Hill "works." The car is Manby-Colegrave's M.G. which he raced with Adrian's tune-up assistance.

selling tuning and overhaul services to racing drivers while the design emerged. By mid-1933 testing of components was underway and in August of 1934 the complete chassis was unveiled. It was sensational. By February 1935 the custom English coach builders, Vanden Plas, had created an aluminum sports body of equal impact and the prototype car X101, pictured here, was ready.

The complete automobile was priced at £1,300 which was *very* expensive for the day; a sporty little Austin "Ulster" with tapering tail and outside ex-

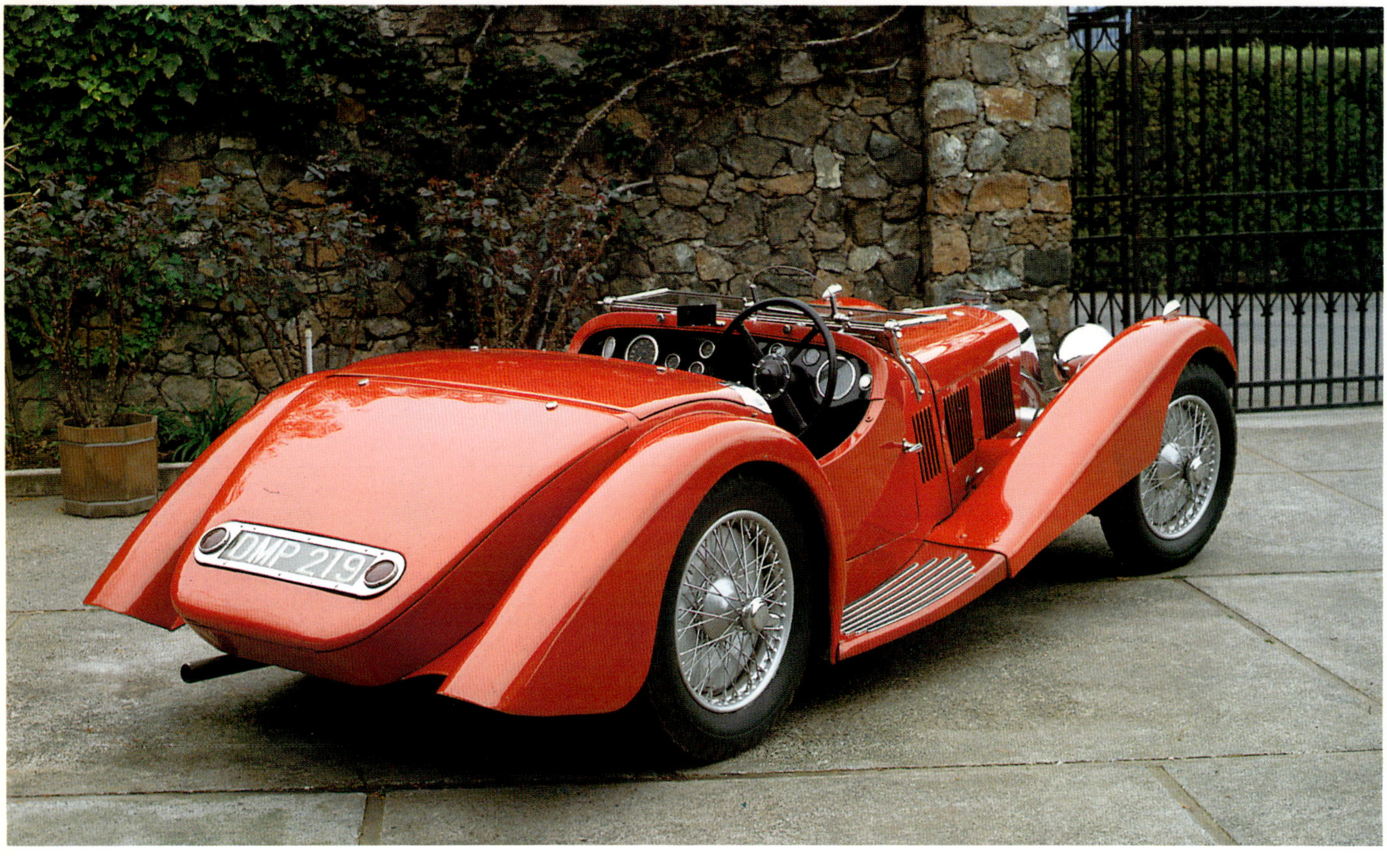

haust could be had for only £185 and the lordly Rolls-Royce with luxury coachwork was little more expensive than the upstart Squire. Adrian was gambling heavily on the better mousetrap theory. Just what was he offering that could command such a sobering price? Simply the best.

Every aspect and specification of the Squire was at the "state of the art" (save the electrical components, alas, provided by Joseph Lucas, the Prince of Darkness). The engine is a 1½ litre, double overhead cam, four cylinder, supercharged lightweight power house. Squire lacked the resources to tool his own engine but he worked closely with the English firm of Anzani to adapt their R-1 engine to his purpose. Anzani was an industrial combine of about the same size as Squire, that is, just a handful of very young and very eager craftsmen. The firm was a descendant of the Italian Anzani company who produced the engine which powered Bleriot in the first flight across the English Channel in 1909. By the early 30's, the English branch had passed through several owners and found itself with little business. The Managing Director, however, was Douglas Ross, a brilliant engineer in his mid-20's. Ross designed the R-1 (for Ross) to capture a share of the sports car market, and Squire became his major (and only) customer when Adrian placed his order for 12 engines. As the relationship between the two firms developed, Ross joined Squire full time to implement the changes in design which Adrian required.

Squire specified an important change in the valve complement by adding rollers to the tappets, but the major change was the addition of a David Brown Roots type supercharger to the front end of the engine. This positive displacement blower operates off the crankshaft and turns at 1½ times engine speed. It boosts to 10 p.s.i. and raises the base horsepower from 70 b.h.p. to 110 at 5,000 r.p.m. Squire had his flying "S" insignia cast into the inlet manifold and crankcase breather caps and the public assumed the entire engine was his design — an error which Squire's sales literature avoided clarifying in spite of the plug, "A Squire deal is a square deal."

Lubrication of this engine is unique. The oil is cooled by passing through a large finned drum filter mounted at the forward end of the chassis for optimum cooling in the airstream. The sump holds two

This photograph shows the Vanden Plas body created for Jock Manby-Colegrave's Squire. The wing treatment is less enveloping but not unattractive.

gallons and is automatically fed fresh oil from a two-gallon tank on the fire wall via a float controlled valve. On the production models this oil tank also incorporates an internal pendulum pump combination which lubricates the springs and joints through piping as the car moves. The Squire is, thus, nearly maintenance free. The engine is started almost silently by a large "dynamotor" which also doubles as the generator; this unit is mounted directly to the crankshaft in front of the engine between the dumb irons and is frequently mistaken for the supercharger. Adrian Squire, as I have said, was an idealist — there is no ignition lock and key. Anyone can flip the ignition toggle switch and drive the car away.

The chassis is relatively strong with X cross members bolted in place. It has to be strong to withstand the stresses imposed by the brakes which are perhaps the car's most outstanding feature. In an era when brakes were frequently dangerously overbalanced by engine power, the Squire-designed brakes were a notable exception. The manganese alloy drums are 15⅛ inches in diameter which, as can be seen in the photos, pretty much fill the entire wheel aperture. They are finned for cooling and actuation is by Lockheed hydraulics. These astonishing brakes are able to bring the car to a dead stop in 20 feet from a speed of 30 m.p.h. — my new Ferrari can't match this performance. The immense bending moments imposed by brakes achieving deceleration of this magnitude could, at the limit, lead to actual fracture of the chassis frame. During the current restoration of X101 by expert Phil Reilly, such cracks were discovered and the chassis has accordingly been further reinforced in the critical areas.

Acceleration of the 2,300 lb. car is excellent. The prototype was tested by the English journal *Motor Sport* in August of 1935 and found to be "striking"; 0 to 60 m.p.h. in exactly 10 seconds with 100 m.p.h. easily achieved at 5,000 r.p.m. But beyond this, road holding was found to be superlative: "fast corners can be taken at 75 m.p.h. as steadily as if the chassis were held by some invisible radius rod." The very low center of gravity, together with straight axles fore and aft, contribute to this effect. Also, the springing and shock absorbers are not stiff so that the ride is quite comfortable.

X101 Squire prototype as shown in an original factory photo. The all aluminum body is by Vanden Plas. The original fenders (one can see why the English call them "wings") were one graceful piece. In later life, some owner modified them into two sections as shown in the color photos; they are now being returned to the original version.

The rapid acceleration is enhanced by the transmission which is a 4-speed E.N.V. Wilson preselector gear box. For better weight distribution Squire mounted this exotic unit well aft of the engine, the power being carried to it via a flexibly mounted shaft. The E.N.V. transmission does not operate in the normal way with a clutch and gearshift lever. Rather, a "pre-selector" knob installed on the steering column is turned to the next gear desired. Nothing happens, however, until a "clutch" pedal is depressed and released, and the shift is then virtually instantaneous. Much, much faster shifts are possible with the Wilson box and one can set up a downshift, as 4th to 3rd, before a corner is reached and have the gear change exactly when needed without the normal distraction. It is an awful lot of fun to play with. Disaster is avoided by requiring the knob to be pulled out before it can be rotated to "reverse"; a tiny pencil beam of light illuminates the knob at night—all was thought of. The Wilson boxes were expensive and used only in thoroughbred automobiles.

Adrian Squire and a stripped racing version at the Brooklands track. The cars raced on a very low budget and achieved only modest results. The best was a third overall in the Mountain Handicap of 1935.

Squire designed both a short chassis (8′6″) and long chassis (10′3″) wheelbase version and showed drawings of beautiful Vanden Plas two- and four-seater closed and drophead bodies in his announcements. The press welcomed the new marque and trumpeted the Squire as the English equivalent of the Bugatti and thousands of inquiries were received at the showroom in Henley. Each car sold was provided with a certificate guaranteeing that it had exceeded 100 m.p.h. at the Brooklands track, and each buyer was assured of a free visit by a Squire mechanic every three months to be sure the car was in top condition. But the better mousetrap just couldn't be sold at Rolls-Royce prices and during the one full year of production only seven cars were purchased, five short chassis and two long. All survive today, although the mechanic no longer pays his quarterly visit.

Squire might have been able to keep going if the economic climate had not been so bleak and if the wretched Jaguar SS 100 had not been introduced in 1936. This imitation sports car cut every corner in

The other side of the car and a further view of the very impressive pre-war Brooklands establishment.

quality and reliability in favor of flashy show, a Jaguar tradition still honored. The "100" designation was supposed to mean 100 m.p.h. which the car could have achieved only in free fall from one of the White Cliffs of Dover—but it cost only £395, under a third of the Squire's price.

The Squire Car Manufacturing Company was at last wound up at a very sad creditor's meeting in July of 1936, and for the next four years Squire returned to work for his mentor, W. O. Bentley, who was then chief engineer at Lagonda. He kept in touch with the old team and was planning a new model for the future. I have a copy of the first Squire sales brochure of 1934. Ironically, it is decorated with a tiny border of swastikas—a symbol for good luck until it later became indelibly associated with Hitler. Adrian Squire's luck ran out for the last time in September, 1940, when he was killed by a German bomb during a raid on the Bristol Aeroplane Company where he had begun working as an engineer. He was 30 years old at the time.

The Squire failed in the marketplace but retains its place in history as the finest English supercharged sports car of the 30's. The first car manufactured, X101 featured in these pages, has spent most of its life in America, having been imported by Charley Davison from the widow of the first owner; he was also killed in the war. Davison, a former official of the Sports Car Club of America, exercised the tough young immigrant against the M.G.'s and Morgans of the early 1950's with great success. The car then passed through several owners until it came to the attention of the late Bill Harrah, the most aggressive of all car collectors. Harrah snapped it up, of course, and it was on display in his enormous museum for some 20 years.

The idea of locking up great cars in a museum has always depressed me. Cars are like yachts which need to be used to exercise their charm and maintain their health. The Harrah collection is a giant automotive prison. During a recent period of confusion over the fate of the collection, the offer for the Squire was accepted and the car was liberated. It is happily back on the road again.

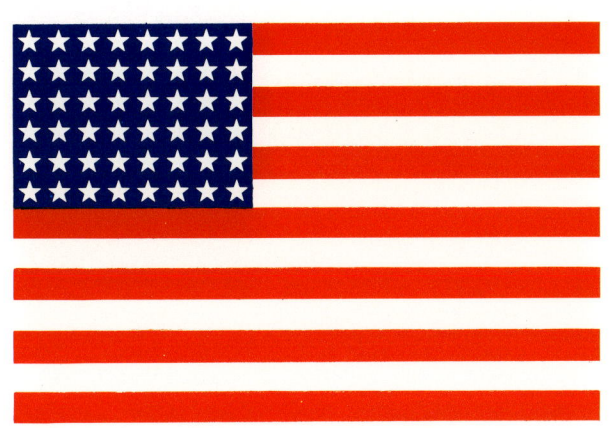

Fred Duesenberg in a rather unnatural and supercilious pose for the photographer.

Maharajadhiraj Raj Rajeshwar Sawai Shree Yashwant Rad Holkar Bahadur of India was a car nut. At 28 the Maharajah had acquired over 30 of the world's finest automobiles at his palace in Indore. Apparently Indian Princing is something of an equipment sport. But life was incomplete; he was missing the most powerful of all, the mighty American supercharged SJ Duesenberg. Moving quickly in 1935, he purchased the last chassis manufactured by that division of the collapsing empire of E. L. Cord and had the long wheelbase (153½ inch) masterpiece shipped from Indianapolis to London where coach builders, J. Gurney Nutting Ltd., had been commissioned to provide a sports body worthy of the dashing young Prince.

The firm, established by Gurney Nutting shortly after the Kaiser war, had become famous for designing the most attractive, if very advanced, coachwork in England. Only Saoutchik of Paris could equal it for flash and flamboyance. Gurney Nutting gave the challenge of the Maharajah's sports car to A. F. McNeil, his brilliant young designer from Scotland, who had already made a name for himself with other

The real Fred Duesenberg at his desk, tired from much genuine hard work.

body designs for royalty. But, what a challenge. This Duesenberg chassis from bumper to tail is nearly 20 feet long! No short chassis (125 inch wheelbase) version like those provided to Gary Cooper and Clark Gable would satisfy the Maharajah. No, the roadster speedster had to be the biggest. It is a tribute to McNeil that he achieved what has come to be considered one of the most beautiful of all Duesenbergs on this huge wheelbase. Only when the car is seen with a person of normal stature standing alongside does one realize how big it really is. Nevertheless, when unveiled at the London Motor Show of 1936, the *Autocar* headline was "People Gasp at the Colossal Car."

The Londoners were also intrigued with various other features of the car—the Maharajah's coat of arms on the doors and his startling choice of colors, "sun-glow" orange and black, for example. But, most commented upon were the six side lights in the wings (fenders)—two white per the regulations, two red and two blue. The red set was to be on when the Prince was at the wheel, and the blue when the Maharanee had her turn. Perhaps it was the contrast of this tre-

DUSIE
NEW YORK
CUW 109

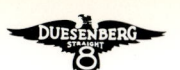

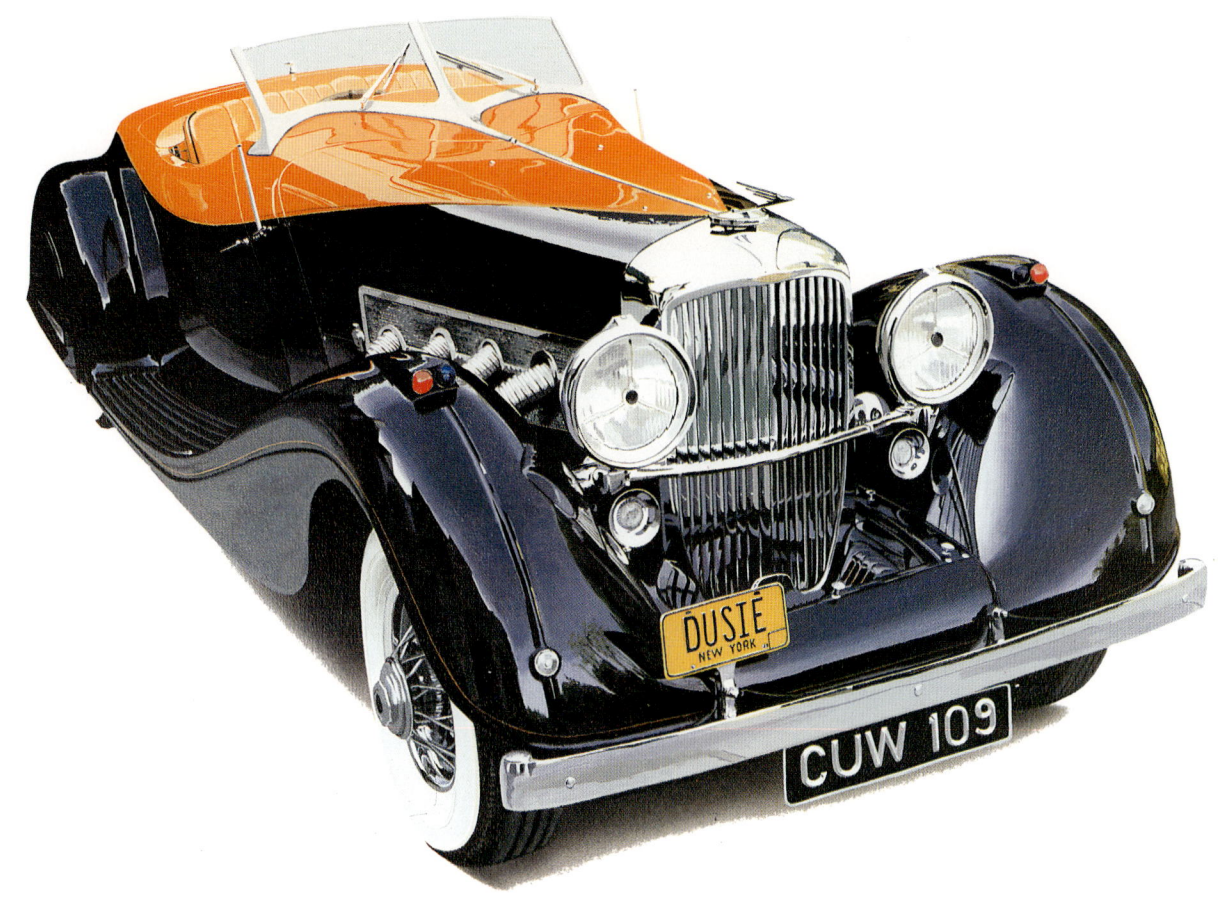

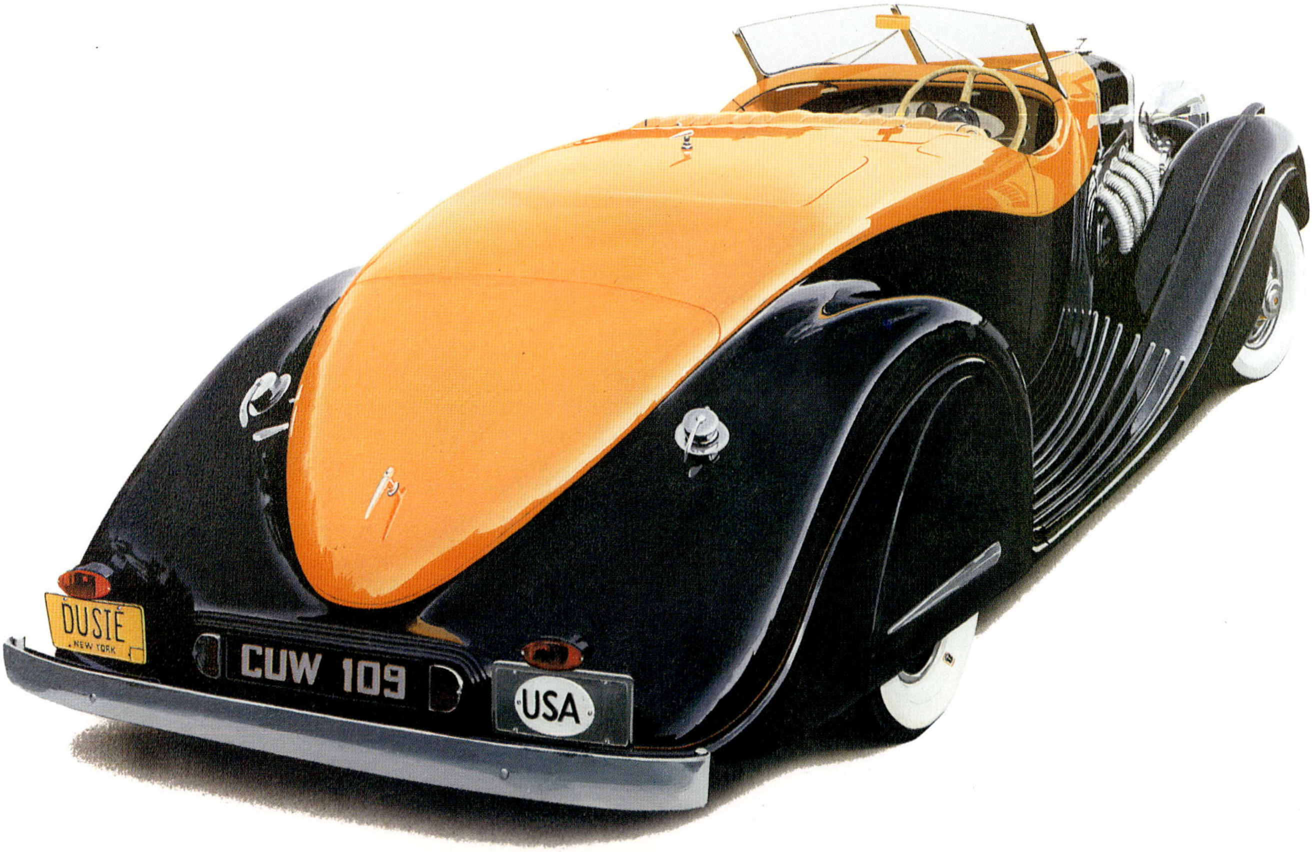
DUSIE
NEW YORK
CUW 109
USA

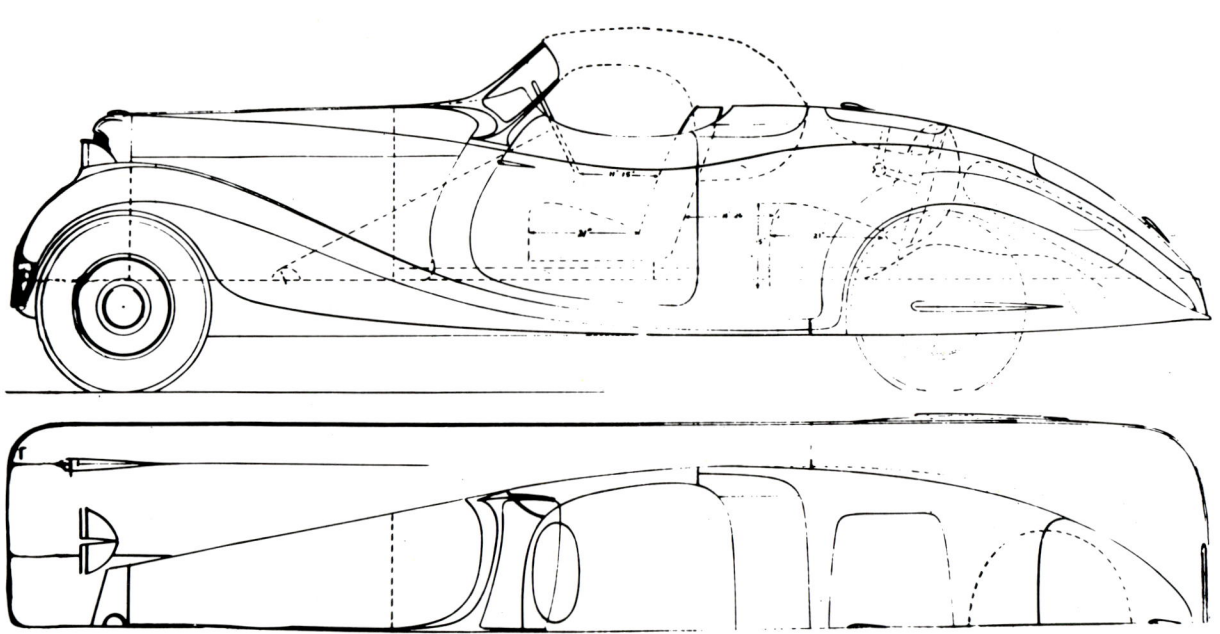

A.F. McNeil's design study for his employer, J. Gurney-Nutting. The Maharajah car is one of the few roadsters from the classic period which looks equally attractive with top up or top down.

mendous car which was the most expensive in the world (over $30,000 1935 dollars) with its royal trappings on its way to India, the poorest nation of all, which provided the most food for thought.

The completed roadster was shipped from London to New York where it was driven back to the factory for the final checkout, after which it drove on to San Francisco to catch the boat for India. As it left the Duesenberg shops in 1936 for the last time, there must not have been many dry eyes among the handful of loyal workers remaining, for the Maharajah's car was the end of the line. America's Duesenberg era was over.

What an era it had been! The Duesenberg broth-

Upon arrival in India, Maharajah Holkar reversed the original color scheme from that of London to a yet more audacious version. Later still, genuine tiger skin upholstery was installed, and the steering wheel was covered with woven rattan.

ers had become famous manufacturing racing cars and the acceptable, if unexciting, Model A. But the Duesenberg age really began when Errett Lobban Cord, the automotive promoter and financier, bought out the company in 1926 and relieved Fred Duesenberg of day-to-day management responsibility and instead gave him the assignment to build the "biggest, fastest and most powerful automobile the world has ever seen." Fred Duesenberg was an engineering genius and he carried out this mission to perfection. The first chassis of the model J was shown at the New York Auto Show on December 1st of 1928, and on that day Duesenberg indeed laid claim to being America's finest.

The engine of the J was among the most sophisticated ever to be incorporated in an automobile. At 6.8 litres and 8 cylinders, it is 4 feet long from fan to flywheel. It has chain-driven double overhead cams with 4 valves per cylinder. The engine is virtually vibration-free thanks to unique cartridges 94% filled with mercury which are incorporated into the crankshaft and dampen normal tortional vibration. Another novel feature is the "timing box" brain which is mounted adjacent to the fuel pump. This box automatically lubricates the entire chassis every 80 miles and alerts the driver to its functioning by flashing a red light on the left of the instrument panel as the pressure plunger begins functioning. A green light below the red advises if the chassis oil reservoir is empty. The timing box also tells the driver via lights on the right side of the panel every 700 miles to change the oil, and every 1,400 miles to add water to the battery.

The standard version of this power plant was claimed to produce 265 horsepower. This was at a time, mind you, when only a few automobiles achieved more than 150 b.h.p.; the famous Packard 12 cylinder engine topped out at 160 b.h.p., for example. In 1932 the SJ engine was introduced which incorporated a water-cooled centrifugal type supercharger running at six times engine speed. This blower raised the pressure to about 8 p.s.i. at 4,000 r.p.m. (a blower speed of 24,000 r.p.m.) and increased the claimed power to 320 b.h.p. In the last few SJ Duesenbergs manufactured (including the Maharajah car), very efficient "ram's horn" induction pipes were fitted which increased the power to

a claimed 400 b.h.p. This SJ engine was for many decades the most powerful automobile motor in the world and, to the best of my knowledge, no car manufactured for street use has its equal today.

The balance of the Duesenberg chassis measures up to the heroic proportions of the engine. The steel frame members are ¼ inch thick and 8½ inches wide at their maximum with ledges of 2¾ inches. Fred believed that only an extremely stiff frame as this could provide the platform required for very high speed stability. The axles are conventional straight members mounted on semi-elliptic springs all around (it was thought that he was planning a radically new chassis with independent suspension at the time of his death in July, 1932, but this never came to pass). The brakes are 15 inches in diameter with wide (3 inch) shoes. They are hydraulic and servo-assisted with a vacuum boost. The Maharajah car is fitted with the standard dial for this servo to accommodate differing road conditions from "dry" to "icy," which must have been useful in India. This brake setup is extremely powerful and there is no hazard in piloting the 2½ ton car even in modern traffic.

The engineering of the Duesenberg was extremely advanced. Aluminum was extensively employed at a time when its use was rather rare and all the exposed aluminum, when highly polished, adds tremendously to the beauty of the mechanical parts. The Duesenberg engine compartment holds its own aesthetically with any of the foreign competition.

Much has been written about the speed potential of this mighty car. The SJ, it was said, would accelerate from zero to 100 m.p.h. in 17 seconds (try this on your modern sports car); 104 m.p.h. was possible in second gear, and with high speed rear axle 140 m.p.h. in third (top) gear was alleged. In 1935 on the Bonneville salt flats a standard SJ chassis with a special streamlined body, indeed, averaged 135 m.p.h. for 24 hours; one hour's average was 152 m.p.h. and the driver, Ab Jenkins, brought the car over the finish line at 160 m.p.h. Yes, but the foreign car advocates will point out that the Duesenberg was so massive, how could it possibly hold its own against the best of the sporty European types?

This question was settled fair and square early one morning in California. The year was 1932 and the Hollywood set was on hand to witness a race be-

D   U   E   S   E   N   B   E   R   G

Duesenberg Power Curve

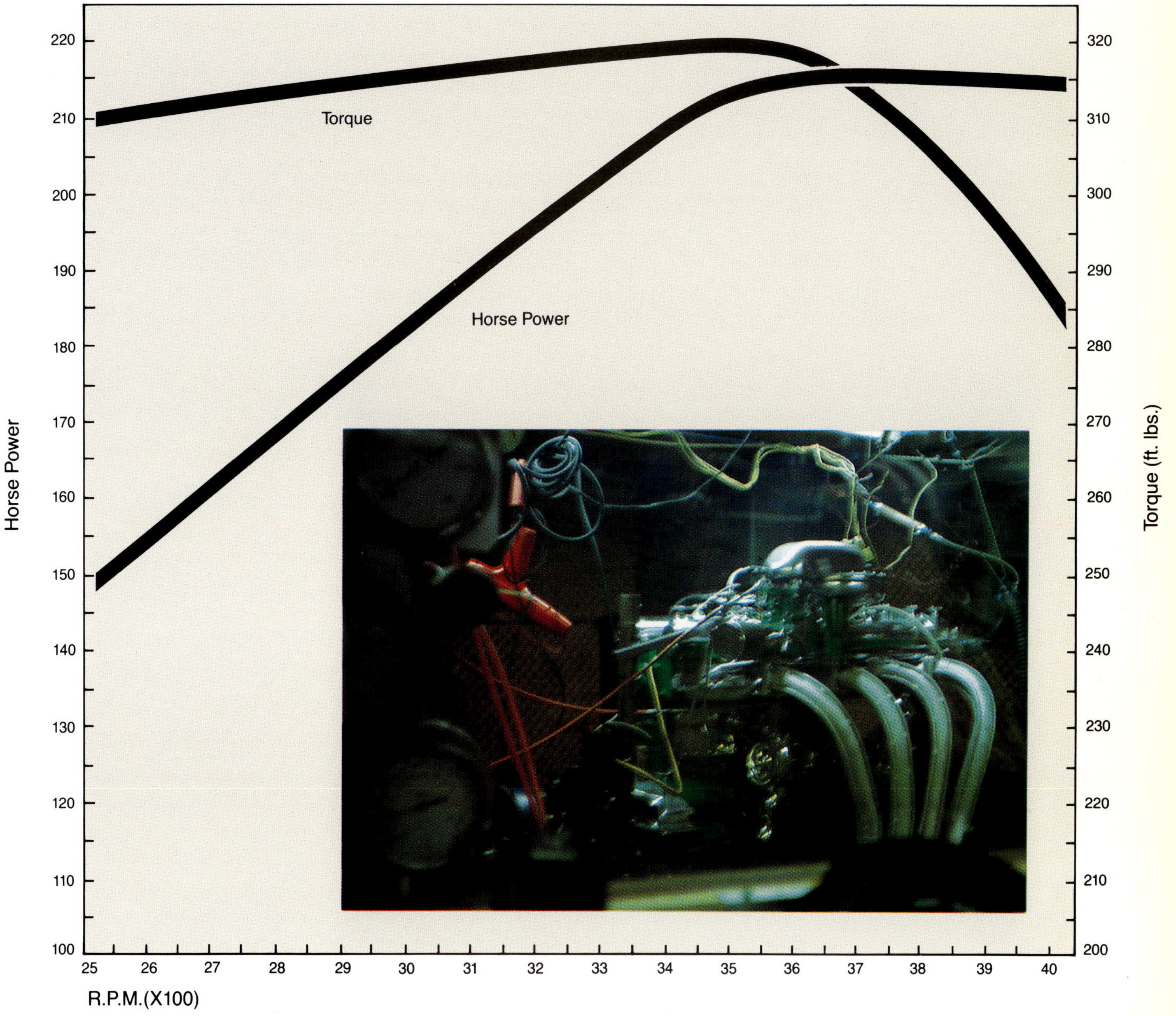

Torque

Horse Power

Horse Power (left axis): 100, 110, 120, 130, 140, 150, 160, 170, 180, 190, 200, 210, 220

Torque (ft. lbs.) (right axis): 200, 210, 220, 230, 240, 250, 260, 270, 280, 290, 300, 310, 320

R.P.M.(X100): 25 26 27 28 29 30 31 32 33 34 35 36 37 38 39 40

The mighty SJ engine was totally overhauled and blue-printed by the Griswold Co. of Berkeley, and dynamometer tested by racing expert Paul Hasselgren. All factory clearance and timing recommendations were observed and double checked with several Duesenberg engine experts. After correction for atmospheric pressure and humidity, full throttle power of 215 b.h.p. was obtained. After normal run-in, another 25 to 40 b.h.p. could be expected. However, measured blower boost was only 3 p.s.i. vs. the 8 p.s.i. of the factory specification. With the full boost, it is conceivable that 300 b.h.p. could be obtained. The advertised SJ power of 320 b.h.p., and particularly the 400 b.h.p. for this late engine with "Ram's Horn" induction pipes, seems unlikely ever to have been achieved without special tuning and special fuel. Nevertheless, the Duesenberg SJ engine is indeed a true "power giant."

*Opposite:
Chassis detail from Ger-
ald Wingrove's 1/15 scale
model of a SJ (super-
charged) Duesenberg.*

95

tween a Duesenberg J belonging to movie mogul Phil Berg and an SSK Mercedes-Benz owned by comic Zeppo Marx (of Marx Brothers fame). A 15-mile, three-lap course was laid out at Muroc Dry Lake Bed on the Mojave Desert east of Los Angeles, and tens of thousands of dollars were wagered on the outcome. Both cars were professionally prepared, tuned to perfection and stripped of exhaust pipes, fenders and all unnecessary weight. Each was driven by an experienced racing driver; it was a serious contest.

The start was at 6:30 in the morning to avoid the blast-furnace heat of later in the day, but in spite of the early hour over a thousand spectators were there to enjoy the spectacle of two of the world's most famous vehicles in combat. After one slow pacing lap, the SSK rapidly out-accelerated the Duesie, but the J caught up after about 3 miles. The Duesenberg driver could hear the scream of the SSK's blower which had to be engaged full time to hold the car in front. That sound was the clue to the outcome. The Duesie had only to keep the pressure on and nature would take its course with the Mercedes. Sure enough, before the end of the second lap horrible things were happening within the SSK's engine under the terrible strain imposed by the supercharger. The SSK slowed, then halted, and the Duesenberg thundered on for the last lap and a decisive victory.

In spite of its prowess, the Duesenberg just could not make it commercially. The car was simply too expensive for the Depression years when a Ford could be purchased for a few hundred dollars. Duesenberg catered to a set symbolized by their ads showing an urbane multi-millionaire type by the helm of his J-class yacht; the only copy: "He drives a Duesenberg." There just weren't enough of these fellows left in 1935. Even at its astronomical price the car had always been a money loser for E. L. Cord who finally had to abandon the wonderful dream. At the end of the era, with the Maharajah's chassis, only some 475 J's had been built including 36 supercharged types; of these, 30 still survive, the finest cars ever produced in America.

The Maharajah's "estate" in India encompassed some 10,000 square *miles;* nevertheless, there weren't many roads so his cars enjoyed relatively light use. After the Hitler war and the social revolution in India, his Duesenberg showed up for sale one Sunday

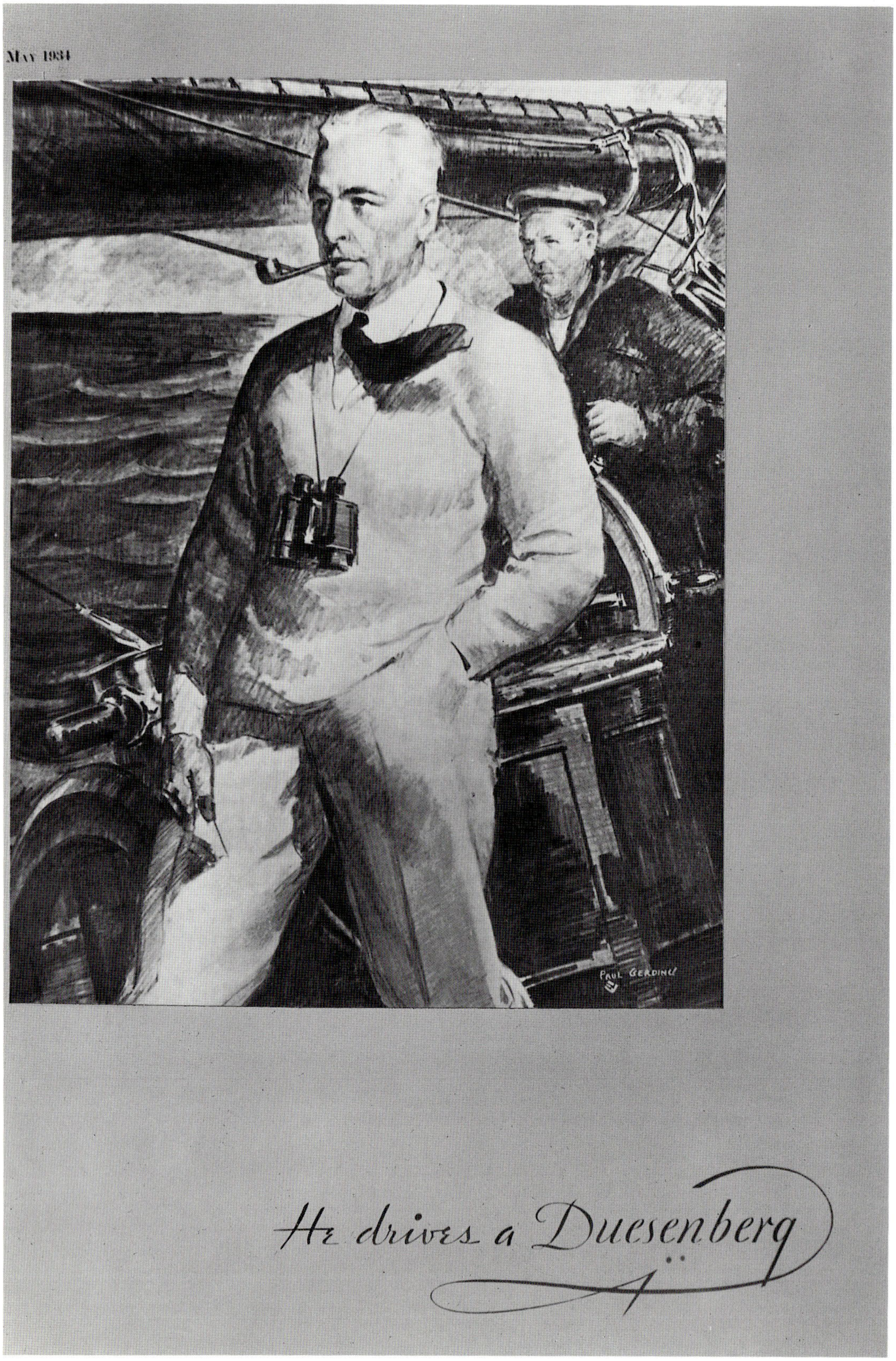

May 1934

PAUL GERDING

He drives a Duesenberg

morning in 1959 in the classified section of the New York Times, with only 8,000 miles use, for "$6,000 cash or a new Cadillac." The dealer was one Sheik Muktar of Bombay who specialized in exporting the classic automobiles accumulated by the various Maharajahs during their heyday of the '20s and '30s. Most of the great automobiles left the country until, almost too late, the Indian Parliament made it illegal to export the classics. The late Duesenberg enthusiast, William Brewster of New York, saw the ad and bought the car sight unseen on probably the best automotive gamble of all time.

Brewster brought the Duesie back to America for a second life. The car was stripped down to its last nut and bolt by Duesenberg expert, Jim Hoe of Connecticut, over a multi-year restoration which was completed in 1964. The magnificent auto was returned to the original perfection it enjoyed when it left the showroom on Lacland Place in 1936. The car promptly won first prize in national Classic Car Club of America competition. After this high point, the SJ was sold and it passed through several American owners receiving some very hard usage in between doing time in both the Ellenville Museum and, after parole, the Auburn-Cord-Duesenberg Museum. Upon arrival in California, it was ready for another thorough rebuild which Autoeuropa has dutifully provided. The car could again pass A. F. McNeil's final inspection at J. Gurney Nutting & Co. Ltd.

This is a sports car in the American idiom; the chassis suits the character of the long straight roads of the Midwest perfectly. But compared to the Alfas and Bugattis, it handles on corners like a truck, a large truck. It is super on the freeway, however, and the visibility over other traffic is wonderful, as the roofs of modern cars come up only to about the door handles on the Duesie. Of course with all that torque, the acceleration is excellent as always, and high speeds are most comfortable.

Recently the Duesenberg has been seen in the company of another of the insatiable Maharajah Holkar's autos ordered at the same time from Gurney Nutting. This is a beautiful Lagonda owned by the great California collector, Jacques Harguideguy. The two cars, to be sure, still sport the double sets of red and blue wing lights, and the happy spirit of the motoring Maharajah lives on.

COMPARATIVE DATA FOR VEHICLES IN THIS BOOK

	Year Made	Cylinders	Valve Mechanism	Valves Per Cylinder	Ignition	Spark Plugs/ Cylinder	Supercharger Type	Capacity	Horsepower
ALFA ROMEO									
Type 6C1750 **Chassis No. 8513064**	'30	6	OHV DOHC	2	Coil	1	Roots	1752 cc	85 bhp
Type 8C2900B **Chassis No. 412019**	'38	8	OHV DOHC	2	Mag	1	Roots	2905 cc	180 bhp
BUGATTI									
Type 55 Roadster **Chassis No. 55229**	'32	8	OHV DOHC	2	Mag	1	Roots	2261 cc	135 bhp
Type 57C Atalante **Chassis No. 57557**	'37	8	OHV DOHC	2	Coil	1	Roots	3257cc	160 bhp
Type 57SC Roadster **Chassis No. 57531**	'36	8	OHV DOHC	2	Mag	1	Roots	3257 cc	200 bhp
Type 57SC Atlantic **Chassis No. 57591**	'38	8	OHV DOHC	2	Mag	1	Roots	3257 cc	200 bhp
DUESENBERG									
Type SJ **Chassis No. 2614**	'35	8	OHV DOHC	4	Coil	1	Water Cooled Centrifugal	6882 cc	400 bhp (Claimed)
MERCEDES-BENZ									
Type SSK **Chassis No. 36038**	'32	6	OHV SOHC	2	Mag & Coil	2	Roots	7065 cc	200/300 bhp
Type 500K **Chassis No. 123702**	'35	8	OHV Pushrod	2	Coil	1	Roots	5019 cc	100/160 bhp
SQUIRE									
Type X101 **Chassis No. X101**	'35	4	OHV DOHC	2	Coil	1	Roots	1496 cc	110 bhp

*FOB London excluding taxes. Multiply by 5 to convert to 1930 dollars.

Wheelbase	Weight	Suspension	Transmission	Brakes	Aprox. Top Speed	Aprox. Price New*	Coachbuilder	Approx. Number Produced	Approx. Number Remaining
108 inches	2072 lbs	Beam Axle	4-speed	Mechanical	95 mph	£1035	Zagato	320 Gran sport	100
110 inches	2400 lbs	IFS IRS	4-speed Transaxle	Hydraulic	120 mph	£2250	Touring	10 Short Chassis	4
108 inches	2645 lbs	Beam Axle	4-speed Mid Frame	Mechanical	112 mph	£1350	Bugatti	38	14
130 inches	2800 lbs	Beam Axle	4-speed	Hydraulic	115 mph	£1400	Bugatti	30	15
117 inches	2300 lbs	Beam Axle	4-speed	Hydraulic	125 mph	£1600	Corsica	1	1
117 inches	2400 lbs	Beam Axle	4-speed	Mechanical	125 mph	£1600	Bugatti	3	3
153 inches	5500 lbs	Beam Axle	3-speed	Hydraulic with Servo	140 mph (Claimed)	£6000	Gurney Nutting	36 (SJ all types)	30
116 inches	3500 lbs	Beam Axle	4-speed	Mechanical	140 mph	£2500	Trossi	31 (SSK)	9
129 inches	5000 lbs	IFS IRS	3-speed with Overdrive	Hydraulic with Servo	103 mph	£2200	Sindelfingen	12 Special Roadster	5
104 inches	2300 lbs	Beam Axle	Wilson ENV 4-speed	Hydraulic	105 mph	£1300	Vanden Plas	5 Short Chassis	5

C R E D I T S

Designed by Marshall Roath and Martha Mann

It is alleged that the author's first word was "car." Be that as it may, he has been a life-long motoring enthusiast having owned, at one time or another, virtually every major sporting marque. He drives the cars in his collection frequently and competes actively in the various classic car events. Trained in both engineering and business, for him the technology of automobiles has been a continuing avocation. A financier and corporate director, the author has been involved with a number of high technology enterprises including major companies in lasers, computers and molecular genetics. He lives with his wife and two children near San Francisco.

The author and his wife receiving the Best of Show award for their Mercedes at the Pebble Beach Concours d'Elegance.

Phototypeset in 12 point Bodoni Book
by Spartan Typographers, Oakland, CA

Manufactured in Japan
by Toppan Printing Co., Ltd., Tokyo